bell hooks

bell hooks

THE LAST INTERVIEW

and OTHER CONVERSATIONS

with an introduction by MIKKI KENDALL

MELVILLE HOUSE
BROOKLYN · LONDON

BELL HOOKS: THE LAST INTERVIEW AND OTHER CONVERSATIONS

First Melville House printing: May 2023

Melville House Publishing   Suite 2000
      46 John Street   and   16/18 Woodford Road
   Brooklyn, NY 11201   London E7 0HA

mhpbooks.com
@melvillehouse

ISBN: 978-1-68589-079-7
ISBN: 978-1-68589-080-3 (EBOOK)

Printed in the United States of America
1   3   5   7   9   10   8   6   4   2

A catalog record for this book is available from the Library of Congress.

CONTENTS

INTRODUCTION

MIKKI KENDALL

> It is my deep belief that in talking about the past, in understanding the things that have happened to us, we can heal and go forward. Some people believe that it is best to put the past behind you, to never speak about the events that have happened that have hurt or wounded us, and this is their way of coping—but coping is not healing. By confronting the past without shame we are free of its hold on us.
>
> —bell hooks, *Teaching Community:*
> *A Pedagogy of Hope*

The evolution of bell hooks from Gloria Jean Watkins (born during Jim Crow to low-income parents) to global feminist icon is a journey that could have come right out of a propaganda film about the American Dream. She attended segregated schools as a child, but as an adult her work was taught in the same institutions that would have denied her entry because of her race and her gender.

Despite being born and raised in a time where Black women were expected to serve and not succeed, hooks defied all expectations and pursued her own dreams. When hooks assumed her pseudonym, taken from the name of her great-grandmother, to honor female legacies, she made a clear statement about who she prioritized as her role models and set herself on the path to becoming a role model for others. In many ways one of the reasons her work resonated with so many is because it tied together the impact and legacy of women's history on the future of women.

I've written in the past about how hooks's work is often an entry point to the academic theories of feminism, shared in a language anyone can understand whether they have a high school education or an advanced degree. Her ideas around race and gender and the impact of stereotypes have been woven deeply into the foundation of modern feminist thought, and yet she largely eschewed celebrity, preferring that the focus be on her words and not on her personally. In this way she spoke to those who might never occupy the spotlight, but who nevertheless wanted to contribute to building the next generation of feminism into something more inclusive and progressive.

In her work hooks also made it clear that to be a feminist was to be in the community, not necessarily as a leader but as a member just like everyone else. As a writer and a Black feminist, hooks was well aware theory was important but theory was not enough, that it was tool for understanding,

"I came to theory because I was hurting," she wrote in her 1991 essay "Theory as Liberatory Practice." "I came to theory desperate, wanting to comprehend—to grasp what was happening around and within me."

Yet hooks didn't shy away from challenging the idea that women couldn't and shouldn't be leaders, pointing out in "Agent of Change: An Interview with bell hooks" that "There are a lot of women out there who are able to lead, and the problem is that people will not follow them." As social movements have shown us time and time again, it is the women who do the work and often the male figureheads who get the credit for the fruits of their unseen labor. The leadership of women is rendered invisible because of the way social movements consciously and unconsciously replicate patriarchal norms. Reading her words on dominator culture and how it harms us in a college class was my turning point with seeing feminism as a movement that could include me.

I came to bell hooks late. I was already in my 20s, already a parent, and firmly fed up with the ways that white middle class feminism Othered me. But I didn't have the right words to express how I felt yet, and so for me reading bell hooks was less revelation and more confirmation. It was maddening to come to feminism as a young Black single mother and find people like me described as a problem to solve with no recognition of our humanity. So, the first time I read *Ain't I a Woman: Black Women and Feminism* I felt seen, more than that I felt validated. It was the feminism that hadn't included me or women like me that was the problem, not my inability to connect with the words of white feminists. Even though they wrote books that were hailed at the time as necessary and relevant reads, hooks made it clear that they were not above critique. As she said in *Feminism is for Everybody: Passionate Politics*, "we knew that there could be no real sisterhood between white women and women of color if white women were not able to divest of white supremacy."

As my own feminism evolved I came to understand that white supremacy, while rooted in misogyny and antiblackness, offers some white women a false idea that tying themselves to white patriarchal power structures would give them power too. It's a siren song of hate, offering strength in being a handmaiden of oppression while obfuscating the reality that there is no equality or equity under the yoke of white supremacy. The reflection of power is about as substantive as moonlight, it provides no warmth, offers no life, it is just easy to romanticize.

When hooks wrote about power and how power relations are built into how we perceive one another, her work validated my personal belief that not looking away, being confrontational, rebelling against demands of being ladylike isn't falling into the stereotype of being an Angry Black Woman, it is instead a way to short-circuit the power dynamics that seek to force women into perpetual subservience. As she talked about in her 1989 interview "Talking Back: Thinking Feminist, Thinking Black":

> It seems to me that we, as women, have a lot of difficulty with the whole issue of assertion of power. I often feel that a lot of the hostility that people feel towards me is that we simply do live in a world where women don't often assert power, and that people get pissed off when women do.

Rejecting the idea that progressive social movements could function in isolation, she tied together feminism, civil rights, and even economics into all her conversations. In the seven interviews in this book, you see how her understanding of these issues deepened across her life and how that thought process is integral to her definition of feminism, as "a movement to end sexism, sexist exploitation, and oppression."

bell hooks changed our understanding of feminism and in doing so, changed the way we talk about everything from children to masculinity. And yet she never took herself too seriously, she understood that part of the work of being human, of being a revolutionary in community and communication with others is to be able to live even as you do the hard necessary work. As she said in a 2015 interview:

We cannot have a meaningful revolution without humor. Every time we see the left or any group trying to move forward politically in a radical way, when they're humorless, they fail. Humor is essential to the integrative balance that we need to deal with diversity and difference and the building of community.

She knew that for a community to be healthy, it had to be happy at some points even if joy was hard to hold onto every day. And that communities started with families, whether they were nuclear, extended, or found. Yet the structure of family, of individuals being present was not enough to tackle current oppression much less create a better future. Through that lens she interrogated the patriarchy not just as an overarching system, but in the way it impacted daily life. Black masculinity was impacted by racism and patriarchy and thus Black families and communities were facing specific struggles. Yet narratives around Black masculinity often focused solely on men with minimal engagement with what it means to be both oppressed and an oppressor. Because hooks centered love in her work, she often highlighted the need for Black masculinity to center love for the self and for others.

In the same vein hooks engaged with hip hop's ideals around Black masculinity and its role in the nuclear family, pushing back against the idea that only a Black male presence was required to make a happy healthy Black family. In an interview with Lawrence Chua, she speaks to her conversations with hip hop icons.

> When I interviewed Ice Cube, he was insisting on the power of the Black father in the home. I was yelling, "Are you really trying to tell me that if you have unloving Black fathers in the home, we're going to have a generation of healthy kids?" Finally, he acknowledged that just having a father present who's not caring is really not going to produce some healthy children. That's the kind of exchange that we should be trying to bring to the floor and not these simplistic representations of sexism and misogyny.

In this way hooks regularly challenged Black culture to not just reinvent itself in the face of outside oppressors, but to consider what was being built and how it would impact the future. Though she did not always agree with the focus of

other Black icons, she largely centered her critiques on impact, challenging thought leaders and artists to consider their
sometimes outsized impact in a society that tried to limit
Black creativity to what would be palatable to white audiences. Creating for more than the white gaze or the male gaze
was the goal.

Reading her interviews, it is clear the work you do, the
work that any of us do, must be rooted in community and
care or it is more likely to be harmful than helpful. For the
world at large bell hooks was less person and more cultural
touchstone. For me, and I suspect lots of other people, she
was someone that made me feel welcomed and wanted and
worthy in an exclusionary space. But like any icon, her place
is less on a pedestal and more in conversation with her work
and how it changed across time. Intent is never more important than impact, and while hooks is widely and right-
fully celebrated, she is as subject to critique as any other icon.
Aware of that reality her interviews also highlight the ways
that her thoughts evolved over time. She never stopped asking
questions of others and of herself. Her opinions on femininity and bodies were sometimes conflicting and even difficult
to absorb, yet she never expected to always be popular. In fact
she often challenged the popular to explain their work, their
image, and their choices beyond what was commercially suc-
cessful. She was comfortable making people uncomfortable,
challenging them to ask hard questions and interrogate the
logic behind their positions.

In this way bell hooks taught us another unforgettable
lesson, that those who do some of the hardest work to make
change possible will have missteps. The mythos that arises

after an icon passes away hinges on their complexities being forgotten in favor of a handful of favorite and easy to absorb quotes. In the way of all icons, when that happens there is a danger of context being forgotten as well. But bell was more than her best quotes, more than her awards and successes, and the best way to honor her work is to think critically about what she said in her time as well as understanding that her experiences may not always be relevant. To remember the full, complicated person she was and learn from her is to wrestle with her growth, her flaws and understand that no feminism, no feminist could ever be perfect. As hooks herself said, "For me, forgiveness and compassion are always linked: how do we hold people accountable for wrongdoing and yet at the same time remain in touch with their humanity enough to believe in their capacity to be transformed?"

bell hooks

FROM
TALKING BACK:
THINKING FEMINIST,
THINKING BLACK

INTERVIEW BY YVONNE ZYLAN
TALKING BACK: THINKING FEMINIST, THINKING BLACK
MARCH 24, 1989

Gloria Watkins was the name hooks used before she adopted her pen name in 1978.

It would not be an exaggeration to say that Gloria Watkins is the focus of a great deal of controversy, criticism, praise and curiosity by nearly all sectors of the Yale community. Both of her classes this year have received double or triple the enrollment expected of them, and a talk given by her at the Law School in February drew so many people it had to be moved to a bigger room, which was still unable to accommodate the crowd. As a student in her Afro-American Literature class last term, I quickly learned that Gloria is not your typical Yale professor. As she herself explains in this interview, she likes to challenge—both others and herself. It is this constant challenging of accepted societal norms that makes Gloria Watkins an inspiring lecturer, a thought-provoking author of radical feminist theory, and a favorite topic of dinner-time conversation.

The following is an interview I had with Gloria on March 24, in which she talked about her books, her lecture at the Law School (which was titled "We Long to Be Loved and We Long to Be Free; We Long to Be Free and We Long to Be Loved."), and her views on "the politics of domination."

YVONNE ZYLAN: You mentioned before that you received a lot of criticism about the absence of a discussion of lesbianism after *Ain't I a Woman* . . .

GLORIA WATKINS: Well, I think it's legitimate critique to raise the question of why there isn't a discussion of lesbianism and it's real complicated. Barbara [Smith] and other people have accused me of homophobia. I remember when I first met Adrienne Rich, she said, "I don't like what you did to lesbians in *Ain't I a Woman*, and I said, "What did I do?" There was the whole sense that I was being homophobic through silencing. I think of homophobia as people who are both afraid of and prejudiced against people who are gay. Certainly silence can be an expression of that. In the case of *Ain't I a Woman*, as you know from reading it, it is a polemical book— I am critical of practically everyone, and needless to say, when lesbians appeared in the book (which they did in the original manuscript) it was in a critical context, and my editor at that time, a lesbian white woman, felt that I should say more positive things about lesbian women. Basically, I was critiquing the whole equation of feminism and lesbianism and also raising the question of whether or not, to some extent, lesbian women have more at stake in the feminist movement in the sense of building culture, and building different places of meeting, etc. Our struggle was that she was saying, "I think if you're going to say these critical things you should say something positive." At that point, I was sick of writing. I mean, this was years of writing, I said, "Uh uh, I don't want to write anything else." But I said, "I realize this is a homophobic culture" and to say critical things about gay people without saying positive things does, in fact, lead you to run the risk of perpetuating homophobia. So I took out every single comment in which the word gay or lesbian was used, and so you have Cheryl Clarke saying about me in *Home Girls* that, you know, bell hooks is so homophobic she can't bring herself to use the word lesbian. I didn't put "lesbian" before their names, does that mean that I'm silencing them? I said, "You know, I didn't put *anyone's* sexual preference before their names . . ." I mean to me these issues are all so complex. I think that there were real ideological differences that kind of got obscured under this more general critique of homophobia.

ZYLAN: Do you think that critique influenced you when you were writing *Feminist Theory: From Margin to Center* because obviously there's a lot more mention of heterosexism and homophobia and how they affect—

WATKINS: I think that one of the things that I had to come to grips with was that everything is a process. I think we have to remember that *Ain't I a Woman*, I started writing it at nineteen . . . I did a lot of the writing of it in Palo Alto and Wisconsin and certainly by the time I came to *Feminist Theory: From Margin to Center*, living in the Bay Area, and having classes of students that were predominantly lesbian, and living part-time with a lesbian couple in San Francisco, I mean my whole perspective had altered in many ways and had, as well, expanded through the whole process of learning and interaction, teaching at San Francisco State. I think a lot of those experiences informed *Feminist Theory: From Margin to Center*. I don't want to make light of the fact that I was really hurt, deeply hurt, as somebody who had always felt, very much, herself to be anti-homophobic and struggling always in day-to-day life to counter homophobia. I was really crushed. I'll never forget that I happened to be particularly down on the day that I went to the bookstore and I saw *Home Girls* and I turned right to that passage where Cheryl Clarke said that I was so homophobic, and I just started screaming, and crying. I felt so hurt that, on the basis of their analysis of this book, people would begin to just make these incredible statements about me as a person . . . I think we all need to be really careful when we fling out labels like this on the basis of something people write, especially something like *Ain't I a Woman*, where the sin has to do with what I didn't say, as opposed to what I did say. Like, for example, not a single person of the people who made these critiques ever called me and said, "Why didn't you have comments about lesbianism in your book?"

ZYLAN: Let's talk a little about your talk at the Law School last month. There was quite a bit of open hostility, at the end during the question-and-answer period, and there seems to be a certain amount of hostility toward the way you approach teaching and the material that you're discussing. You talked in . . . *Margin to Center* about, time after time, where there's hostility and anger and tears, that can be an effective way of changing or helping somebody or yourself to come to a new perspective. Is there a conscious attempt on your part to spark that kind of confrontation?

WATKINS: Not at all. There *is* always a conscious attempt on my part to challenge. I mean there is not a day of my life that

I am not critiquing myself and looking at myself to see if my politics are borne out in the way that I live and the way that I talk and present myself. I think that one of the best readings of *Ain't I a Woman* for me came from a white woman student at Santa Cruz, a graduate student, Katie King, who said that, what she felt was that what I was always asking of people was that they shift their paradigms, and that whenever you ask people to shift their paradigms, they respond with hostility. I did not ever feel that I was hostile [at the Law School talk]. I feel that I very much asserted power, and I don't feel that I asserted it with the intent to dominate, but I did assert it. It seems to me that we, as women, have a lot of difficulty with the whole issue of assertion of power. I often feel that a lot of the hostility that people feel towards me is that we simply do live in a world where women don't often assert power, and that people get pissed off when women do. I feel that women particularly are not allowed to be non-nurturing in our styles. I mean, people will praise male professors who have eccentric styles, or what have you, but those same characteristics in a woman become subject to real scrutiny and critique. I feel like in the talk I had been very open, very compassionate and very vulnerable. I was none of those things in the question-and-answer period. I was fatigued, and as I became fatigued, I became less willing to take on the whole burden of the discussion. One of the things I said was that in most cases I tried to throw people's questions back to them, but see, there again, we work within a paradigm where, usually, speakers are very nurturing during question-and-answer periods, very receptive, or they put on an air of receptivity, and I didn't put on an air of receptivity at all. I was surprised at myself, in that I've never felt such a split before, but I think that the *talk* was very difficult for me. I think that people did not really cut me a great deal of slack in terms of the difficulty of talking about male domination at a place where people are certainly not talking about male domination every day, and the difficulty of giving a paper at a place where you talk about your personal life as well—how many people try to integrate personal experience with their theoretical and analytical work here? Not many. All of those things made that talk very, very stressful. It's interesting to me that I said several times before the talk, even, that I was tired, but that did not in any way cause people to shift their expectations. I was impressed by the fact that most of the feedback I got was about the question-and-answer period and not the talk itself.

ZYLAN: Do you find that that's often the case, that the way you present something deflects attention away from what you're saying?

WATKINS: Yes, and I think we have to be really suspicious of that—people don't want to deal with male domination—how convenient to turn a discussion of male domination into a critique of me. Just recently I gave a talk at a Black women's film festival, and it was interesting, because the topic was supposed to be on Black women and finding a Black female voice. The audience and the panel members never focused on Black women. But that seems logical in a culture where Black women are at the very bottom of the social and economic totem pole. And so I had to say to people that they would have to take a minute and examine how we're interacting here because every time the topic of Black women comes up, we switch it to something else. I wanted us to examine what was our own difficulty in actually talking about Black women, in taking the Black woman's experience seriously. It seems to me that this happens a lot with feminist concerns. People deflect away from them in all kinds of ways.

ZYLAN: You talked in *Ain't I a Woman* and in . . . *From Margin to Center* about the question that people are always asking you: Which is more important to a Black woman, a question of racism or a question of sexism? And you seem to be making the point that they are interlocked and are of equal importance, and yet, in some of your arguments, there's a sense of primacy to questions of racism, that it is more endemic to our society, the structures which dominate and oppress people.

WATKINS: Well, one of the things that I definitely tried to say is that we've seen a great many more structural changes in the position of women, and especially white women, and privileged women in our culture than we could say about race. Certainly feminist struggle is not nearly as old as the struggle against racism in this culture. I think to say that they are of equal importance does not belie the fact that there are also occasions in which one may be more important. I mean, as I grow older, I find that issues of sexism and gender domination obsess my psyche a lot more and that's because a lot of the kinds of things that I've struggled with around race have become, as I have established myself, less problematic than interpersonal issues of domination, etc. And I think we ought to be willing to allow for the possibility that at different moments in one's life, one issue has primacy over another.

ZYLAN: In . . . *Margin* you talk about the things that are
divisive in terms of "sisterhood" and the false sense of bonding upon shared oppression, but isn't that shared oppression,
or that perception of shared oppression what brings women
together around feminism in the first place? Isn't it necessary?

WATKINS: It doesn't seem to be, Yvonne, in terms of Black
and white women, because our senses of oppression are so
different. Or let's say, white women and women of color. I
think that, again, it's a kind of complex thing. I think back
to some of the sessions I've had in the past week, where
groups of us as Black women sat around and talked about
different things that were going on in our lives. There was
a sense of bonding because of the similarity of those experiences, but I think that if there had been a white woman in
the room, the sense of that sharedness would have changed,
because a lot of what we were talking about was influenced
by both race and sex oppression. One can, of course, find
a basis of bonding in shared experience and shared experience of oppression, but that is not the kind of bonding that
will really transcend race, class, and ethnic lines. I think
that is one form of bonding that can still exist for us, but I
think we have to insist on a bonding that is about political
commitment to feminism. And, I tell you, having come out
of a strong feminist context, both in living experience and
work experience, in California, to here—when I get into
non-feminist environments, the difference is so incredible
to me. I mean, I was on a panel recently with two women
who were not committed to feminism—this made such a

difference in how we dealt with each other as women and how the discussion went. To me, it's really wonderful and beautiful to bond with women in shared commitment to feminism—and with men.

ZYLAN: It seems that one thing that comes up repeatedly in your arguments is the idea that bourgeois white women, who were involved in organizing contemporary feminism, taking control, etc., became involved in feminism as a means to get access to the privileges that only men could enjoy in the capitalist system. You talk about women who are in power not doing anything different with that power; they're doing what men do . . . Do you think that this is some fundamental flaw in contemporary feminism, that it was founded as a vehicle for getting more out of the capitalist system for women?

WATKINS: I think that it's important that people read works like Zillah Eisenstein's *The Radical Future of Liberal Feminism* that try to document for us the fact that it's a liberal movement and that it places a great deal of emphasis on reform. I mean, the Civil Rights Movement, as well, placed a great deal of emphasis on reform. And I think it has been a tradition that, other than Communist or other anti-capitalist movements, most reform movements under capitalism have had as a basic intent that one will struggle for some of the privileges that those in power have. So, in this way, I don't see [the] contemporary feminist movement as unique, but at the same time, I think it was, tremendously, a basis of a movement that would automatically exclude a great many people. I mean, look at some of the symbolic gestures we see naming the beginning of the movement: the bra-burning, protesting the Miss America Pageant . . . What if our symbolic gestures were women at a factory protesting working conditions? This would have a far more radical impact on our consciousness than the image of people burning a bra or some of the other symbolic gestures that came to be seen by popular media as indications of the direction of [the] feminist movement. And though people would say, "Well, that isn't what it was ever about," that isn't even important, if those become the symbols that the mass audience of people know. In a sense, if that's how people perceive feminism, we still have to deal with that. Why didn't we want other symbols that would have been more striking to us, in terms of their political intent.

ZYLAN: You did critique in . . . *Margin to Center* Zillah Eisenstein's contention that there is radical potential in liberal feminism. Do you think that there isn't because of that kind of . . .

WATKINS: Well, I don't think that there's radical potential in any movement where people imagine that we can hold onto class privilege under capitalism and have radical change. I think there's a lot of useful stuff in Zillah's book, but I simply don't see the bearing out of the ideas that she sets forth, because, theoretically, if she were right in her analysis, we would be witnessing this radical breakthrough, and what we're witnessing is just the opposite, a regression. A moving away from feminist concerns, as opposed to an aggressive push to radicalism that she implied in that text.

ZYLAN: In your chapter "Rethinking the Nature of Work," you talked about the fact that there's no appeal in this idea of women going out and getting jobs to liberate themselves— for poor women, non-white women, lower-class women. Is this an indication that there is no value in women who do not hold paying jobs establishing some amount of economic independence? Or is there no liberatory potential in work, given the capitalist context?

WATKINS: The primary thing I was trying to say is that, for people who work for very low wages, there is no economic self-sufficiency to be found in work. The fact is, you make just enough to get by, so the sense that you are actually working toward something that will allow you to have a degree of free- dom of movement or freedom of options, material options or otherwise, just isn't there for people. There's not the sense that work is really going to liberate you to have some time. Let's say you've been in a marriage, where you work part-time and you feel oppressed in that marriage, but your income joined with that of your spouse allows you some time: some time to go shopping, some time to go for a walk in the park, some time to read. What's going to motivate you to want to give that up—even though you may feel oppressed, or depressed, or repressed in that marriage—for a situation where you're going to have to work so many more hours per week and not have any kind of economic flexibility or time flexibility? There was a sort of lie in the fact that so much of the emphasis on work within the feminist movement really had to do with careers, which are by their very nature so different from the kind of work most people do. If you come into the workforce with a PhD, or other skills that you can utilize, you're not talking about getting a very low-paying job for forty hours a week. In my own life, coming from years of making a very low wage, because I've been working part-time for the last, what, five or six years, it's exciting to [now] make a wage that gives me flexibility, where I can send some money home, or take a trip, or do something. That kind of work is, I think, experienced by people as liberatory. But the kind of work you do where you do it and at the end of the month you still don't have any money, your life hasn't altered in any kind of significant way, you just simply don't experience that as liberatory. [*pause . . . laughter*] Make sure you put this laughter in. [*more laughter*]

ZYLAN: You discuss the divisive effect of classism, racism, and sexism on female solidarity, and I don't want to beat this into the ground, but what about heterosexism? It seems to be conspicuously absent . . .

WATKINS: Well, now, I've had a lot of arguments with people about this. I feel that a critique of heterosexism, to me, is included in the notion of sexism. I don't see heterosexism as being a separate category, because it seems to me that heterosexism is definitely the child of sexism. It is the child of gender oppression. I mean, when I think about sexism as a sort of general category of patriarchy, I do tend to think of there being all these subheadings, like homophobia. I mean, if you want to have this little world where men and women marry as part of your sexist vision, then it just seems to me that homophobia will necessarily be one of the modes of thought that you will encourage. I've had arguments with people who have felt very strongly that it simply isn't covered by that. I think that we haven't insisted on the reality that heterosexism is a central dimension of what sexism is.

ZYLAN: But doesn't it, in its specific manifestations, in terms of its divisiveness between women, merit some *explicit* mention—

WATKINS: Yes, I think that certainly the arguments I made would have been strengthened by talking about that . . . I like very much the terms "woman-identified" and "male-identified," and not in terms of them as indicative of sexual preference, but in terms of who you place at the center of your actions, your sense of self, or what have you. I remember [in one of my classes in California] in which students were lamenting that I did not have a lesbian identity and some of the students were saying that they felt really bad because they felt that a strong feminist like myself should be a lesbian. Betty, the Black lesbian woman that I lived with, said, "Gloria is a woman-identified woman whose affectional interests lie with a man." I think that the general sense of feeling care for *all* women, that whenever you see a woman in distress you feel some sense of unity, is what I think of when I think of being woman-identified. Whenever I'm in non-feminist circles, speaking, I can really get a sense of what that is, in terms of women taking care of women, in terms of women *acknowledging* women. At this one conference I was at recently, I was struck by how the different women panel members never looked at one another. They would look directly at men, and talk to men and cater to the interests of men, etc. If we had all been woman-identified in that room [at the Black women's film festival] we wouldn't been struggling around the issue of why we couldn't place Black women at the center of the discourse. The sense that "the real feminist is a lesbian" came out of that whole feeling about what it means to be woman-identified. As you probably know, there are many lesbian women who do not feel that sense of political solidarity with women.

ZYLAN: And you discussed in your [Law School] talk about the lesbian who dresses like a man, and takes on those accoutrements of power. Is that the male-identified woman?

WATKINS: Well, I used to, with good buddies, talk about these women, we used to call them "daddy's girls" because a lot of them were women who grew up identifying with their fathers and really, actually, hating their mothers. I mean, I know one of those women who used to say always that she just couldn't stand her mother's helplessness, and her role model of power was from her father. And these women can be found around—they may have sex with women, but a lot of their good buddies are males, and in fact they feel stronger identification with males than with women. And in a sense, they become honorary males who, like men, sleep with women, but who in a sense don't have a feeling of overall respect for women, and in fact may have a tremendous sense of contempt toward any woman who does not have the same style of strength and assertiveness, etc., etc. I remember the period of my life when I thought I wanted people to take me more seriously, as an undergraduate. I felt the real need to like, have short hair, and to wear a certain kind of clothing that did not suggest sensuality or sexuality. I mean, one of the things that I would say is that most male clothing does not evoke sexuality or sensuality, especially if we think about the colors of male clothing. Take, say, the business suit as a symbol, a clothing symbol of male power or even, say, the kind of clothing I was talking about in my talk, the uniforms of working-class men. My father was a janitor at the post office in our town for more than about thirty years and the clothing he wore was always drab. There's no suggestion of sexuality and sensuality in that clothing. In a sense, one of the things that we know is that it is the role of women to be sexual and sensual, and it is the role of men, that is, under patriarchy and within sexism, to conquer that sexuality. It's embedded as a signifier in the clothing that we wear. I know when I wanted to be taken seriously as a thinking, intellectual young woman, I felt the need to sort of destroy those signs of sensuality and sexuality in my clothing. It was really a great moment for me (because you know how interested I am in fashion) when I was in Spain, in Barcelona, one night a couple of summers ago, and the garbage collectors were out. They were all wearing bright orange uniforms and I was so thrilled. I remember growing up and never liking the garbage collectors because I saw them as somehow dirty people. One of the many articles I want to write about fashion has to do with how much in this culture we sort of make the job a person's identity. And I was so happy when I saw these men because they looked bright, they looked cheery, they looked like people you could look at. Usually their garb is sort of gray and drab and not something that is inviting, because it is not something that separates them from the task that they are doing and reminds us of their humanity and their dignity as people.

ZYLAN: A lot of your analysis comes back to how capitalism underlies systems of oppression (correct me if I'm wrong), so is it a question of dismantling capitalism or is it a question of dismantling each of the systems of oppression . . .?

WATKINS: Well, yeah, I was going to disagree with you. I think that a lot of my analysis comes back to an insistence upon interlocking systems of domination, something that I occasionally refer to as a "politic of domination." I think that capitalism is simply one manifestation of that politic of domination. I think that any form of socialism that places material values over human values can be equally integrated into a system of domination, so that I don't think that capitalism is the sole evil, let's eliminate it . . . but certainly I think that it is a central part of this system of domination that has to be dismantled.

ZYLAN: So, when you are talking about a "politic of domination," that refers to all these interlocking systems of oppression—

WATKINS: And it also refers to the ideological ground that they share, which is a belief in domination, and a belief in notions of superior and inferior, which are components of all of those systems. For me it's like a house; they share the foundation, but the foundation is the ideological beliefs around which notions of domination are constructed. One of them, which I talk a lot about, certainly, in class, is Western metaphysical dualism. The whole notion of good, bad, evil, the triumph of good over evil and all of those kinds of notions.

ZYLAN: What about the question that was asked at the end of your Law School talk, by Matt [Hamabata—professor of sociology]: Why should men want to change; I mean what have they got invested in it?

WATKINS: You know, the thing that really got me about that question, I thought about it for days, is that so many people expressed this real hard-core sense that men are never going to change. And I thought, can you imagine the despair of Black people under slavery had we felt that there was nothing about that system that was going to change, that there was nothing about white people as a group, or as individuals, that would change? And it seems to me that, one of my favorite, favorite statements that I say a lot, which I didn't say that night because I was too tired, is the whole notion that "what we can't imagine, can't come to be." I feel like we've got to believe that men can change, and I believe profoundly that we have individual incidents of men changing. We can't discredit that reality by insisting there is nothing at stake for these people, that there is no hope that they will change. I mean, in a sense, it was very ironic that Matthew Hamabata would be asking this question. The very fact that a man such as he could be born into this world in an environment that was conducive to his identifying with women and with the struggle of women for liberation, to me, is a signifier of the possibility for change.

ZYLAN: Well, then Matt continued his question, after you made the comparison of white people having changed, and he said, "Well, I don't see white people giving up the reigns

of power, really . . ." There may be huge changes, but still the
white-supremacist, capitalist patriarchy remains intact.

WATKINS: This is true. But I don't think that means that we're
going to stop resisting that system, or that we're going to give
up hope that it won't alter itself, or that it won't be altered, let
us say, because it's not going to alter itself. And I don't think
that one has to also see change as necessarily those in privilege giving up privilege. It may be those in privilege having
that privilege taken away from them by the masses of people
who don't share. And certainly, in revolutionary struggles all
around the planet, we see this happening. We see a commitment on the part of oppressed peoples, certainly in places like
Nicaragua and El Salvador, to struggle, and to make life very
different and very difficult for those in privilege who oppress.
But the talk was saying that there are men who are in pain,
and it seems to me that feminist change could be a way out of
that pain. Now, whether or not men will take that way out, I
think that I would tend to feel very negatively about that. But
I still think that we have to insist upon this as a space and a
place for change.

AGENT OF CHANGE: AN INTERVIEW WITH BELL HOOKS

INTERVIEW BY HELEN TWORKOV
TRICYCLE: THE BUDDHIST REVIEW
FALL 1992

bell hooks is a seeker, a feminist, a social critic, and a prolific writer. Her books include *Ain't I a Woman: Black Women and Feminism*; *Talking Back: Thinking Feminist, Thinking Black*; *Breaking Bread: Insurgent Black Intellectual Life* (with Cornel West); and, most recently *Black Looks*, all from South End Press.

She was born Gloria Watkins forty years ago in Hopkinsville, Kentucky, and was educated at Stanford and Yale. Currently she teaches English and Women's Studies at Oberlin College in Ohio. This interview was conducted for *Tricycle* by editor Helen Tworkov.

HELEN TWORKOV: What was your first exposure to Buddhism?

BELL HOOKS: When I was eighteen I was an undergraduate at Stanford and a poet, and I met Gary Snyder. I already knew that he was involved with Zen from his work, and he invited me to the Ring of Bones Zendo for a May Day celebration. There were two or three American Buddhist nuns there and they made a tremendous impression. Since that time I've been engaged in the contemplative traditions of Buddhism in one way or another.

TWORKOV: And that excludes Nichiren Shoshu? Which is the only Buddhist organization in America with a substantial Black membership?

HOOKS: Yes, Tina Turner Buddhism. Get-what-you-want Buddhism—that is the image of Buddhism most familiar to masses of Black people. The kind of Buddhism that engages me most is about how you're going to live simply, not about how you're going to get all sorts of things.

TWORKOV: How do you understand the absence of Black membership in contemplative Buddhist traditions?

HOOKS: Many teachers speak of needing to have something in the first place before you can give it up. This has communicated that the teachings were for the materially privileged and those preoccupied with their own comforts. When other Black people come to my house they say, "Giving up what comforts?" For Black people, the literature of Buddhism has been exclusive. It allowed a lot of people to say, "That has nothing to do with me." Many people see the contemplative traditions—specifically those from Asia—as being for privileged white people.

TWORKOV: We find references and quotes from Vietnamese Zen master Thich Nhat Hanh throughout your work. Is part of your attraction to him his integration of contemplation and political activism?

HOOKS: Yes. Nhat Hanh's Buddhism isn't framed from a

location of privilege, but from a location of deep anguish—the anguish of a people being destroyed in a genocidal war.

TWORKOV: In addition to Thich Nhat Hanh, the Buddhist references in your work extend to those books that fall into the category you defined as exclusive. How did you get past that?

HOOKS: If I were really asked to define myself, I wouldn't start with race; I wouldn't start with blackness; I wouldn't start with gender; I wouldn't start with feminism. I would start with stripping down to what fundamentally informs my life, which is that I'm a seeker on the path. I think of feminism, and I think of anti-racist struggles as part of it. But where I stand spiritually is, steadfastly, on a path about love.

TWORKOV: Does it have a name?

HOOKS: If love is really the active practice—Buddhist, Christian, or Islamic mysticism—it requires the notion of being a lover, of being in love with the universe. That's what Joanna Macy talks about in *World as Lover, World as Self* (Parallax, 1991). Thomas Merton also speaks of love for God in these terms. To commit to love is fundamentally to commit to a life beyond dualism. That's why love is so sacred in a culture of domination, because it simply begins to erode your dualisms: dualisms of black and white, male and female, right and wrong.

TWORKOV: Considering your critiques of the sexist, racist patriarchy, this path of love is pretty challenging.

HOOKS: That's why I enjoyed Stephen Butterfield's article (in *Tricycle*, Vol. i, Number 4) dealing with sexual ethics and Buddhist practice—precisely because he said, "Let's leave this discourse of right and wrong, and let's talk about a discourse of practice." Something may in fact work for one person, and may be fundamentally wrong for another, and that's complex. If I'm a teacher and you enter this room, it's a lot more difficult to think about what would be essentially useful to you than to think what the rules are. That's about love, and I think that's what Butterfield tries to say in talking about passion. Teacher/student relationships are arenas for disrupting our addiction to dualism, and we are called upon to really strip ourselves down, to where we don't have guides anymore. In real love, real union, or communion, there are no rules.

TWORKOV: As a prominent Black feminist, how difficult is it for women, especially other Black feminists, to hear you say that your fundamental sense of yourself is as a seeker on the path? Does it evoke a sense of betrayal?

HOOKS: I think so, certainly a few years ago it did. But feminists in general have come to rethink spirituality. Ten years ago if you talked about humility, people would say, I feel as a woman I've been humble enough, I don't want to try to erase the ego—I'm trying to get an ego. But now, the achievements that women have made in all areas of life have brought home the reality that we are as corruptible as anybody else. That shared possibility of corruptibility makes us confront the realm of ego in a new way. We've gone past the period when the rhetoric of victimization within feminist thinking was so complete that the idea that women had agency, which could be asserted in destructive ways, could not be acknowledged. And some people still don't want to hear it.

TWORKOV: To what extent has the issue of victimization in feminism been diffused by the national obsession with—as you call it—victimage?

HOOKS: In a culture of domination, preoccupation with victimage is inevitable.

TWORKOV: And this keeps dualities locked in place?

HOOKS: I used to believe that progressive people could critique the dualities and dissolve them through the process of deconstruction. But that turns out not to be true. With the resurgence of forms of Black nationalism that say white people are bad, Black people are good, we see an attachment to notions of inferiority. Dualities serve their own interests.

TWORKOV: How does this come up for you in your daily life?

HOOKS: Life was easier when I felt that I could trust another Black person more than I could trust a white person. To face the reality that this is simply not so is a much harder way to live in the world. What's scary to me now is to see so many people wanting to return to those simplistic choices. People of all persuasions are feeling that if I don't have this dualism,

I don't have anything to hold on to. People concerned with dissolving these apparent dualities have to identify anchors to hold on to in the midst of fragmentation, in the midst of a loss of grounding.

TWORKOV: Your anchor is love?

HOOKS: Yes. Love and the understanding that things are always more complex than they seem. That's more useful and more difficult than the idea that there is a right and wrong, or a good or bad, and you just decide what side you're on.

TWORKOV: We see this in your relationship with Thich Nhat Hanh. You quote him with obvious reverence, but not with blind devotion. You have also referred to gender-related problems with his teaching.

HOOKS: When Nhat Hanh is talking about work or our engagement in social issues, his vision is so vast, so inclusive, so generous. But on questions of family and marriage and sex, we get the most conventional notion of what's good. Celibacy is good or having a family is good. There's nothing between celibacy and family life.

TWORKOV: I've been puzzled by the same contradiction in his work. But I've wondered if it's a contemporary pragmatic response to the lives of his students.

HOOKS: One of the threads that I see in all his writing is a particular kind of memory of childhood that he holds to: a childhood of pre-awareness of anguish, one might say. He evokes the child as an aware being but it's the child who has no anguish and no sense of horror. And in his romantization of the heterosexual family—which is always biased—it's very clear that it remains biased in favor of the old order of patri-archy and hierarchy.

TWORKOV: Have you ever met Thich Nhat Hanh?

HOOKS: I've been afraid to. As long as I keep a distance from that thread, I can keep him—and I can critique myself on this—as a kind of perfect teacher. Reading about his attachment to certain sexist thinking in a book is one thing, but actually expe-riencing it at a gathering would be another thing. That would be sad for me. I want his wisdom to extend into his thinking about family and gender relations or sexuality, and I don't see that.

TWORKOV: Do you see it anywhere?

HOOKS: Trungpa Rinpoche's thinking is still the most pro-gressive in terms of desire and sexuality. Whether he was able to live those theories out in their most expansive possibility is another thing. What I get from him and Merton, that I don't get from Nhat Hanh, is a real willingness to think of pleasure as a potential site of spiritual awakening and enlightenment. Thich Nhat Hanh cuts off sensual pleasure from any con-tinuum that would lead to desire and to sexuality.

TWORKOV: In your interview with Andrea Juno (in *An-gry Women* [Re/Search, 1992]) you talk of having been a cross-dresser, which, for women is, among other possibilities, a foray into the dominant culture. How does it experiment with the deconstruction of the self and, simultaneously, with the patriarchy?

HOOKS: I thought of it as an experience of erasure. When Joan of Arc erased herself as female, she was also trying to erase the self to which she was most attached. And her experience of cross-dressing was a path leading her away from the ego-identified self. She didn't replace one attachment with another—"Now I'm the identity of a man." It was more, "Now I'm away from the identity I was most attached to."

TWORKOV: This is the same kind of experimentation as using your grandmother's name—bell hooks—for writing?

HOOKS: I think so. It's primarily about an idea of distance. The name "bell hooks" was a way for me to distance myself from the identity that I most cling to, which is Gloria Watkins, and to create this other self. Not dissimilar really to the new names that accompany all ordinations in Muslim, Buddhist, Catholic traditions. Everyone in my life calls me Gloria. When I do things that involve work, they will often speak of me as "bell," but part of it has been a practice of not being attached to either of those.

TWORKOV: As in: "I'm not trying to be bell hooks."

HOOKS: The point isn't to stay fixed in any role, but to be committed to movement. That's what I like about notions in Islamic mysticism that say, "Are you ready to cut off your head?" It's like asking, "Are you ready to make whatever move is necessary for union with the divine?" And that those moves may be quite different from what people think they should be.

TWORKOV: What would you say is the Buddhist priority? What are our moves?

HOOKS: I think one goes more deeply into practice as action in the world and that's what I think when I think about engaged Buddhism.

TWORKOV: Are you making any distinctions here between Thich Nhat Hanh's use of the expression "engaged Buddhism" and "liberation theology"?

HOOKS: No. I like that the point of convergence of liberation theology, Islamic mysticism, and engaged Buddhism is the sense of love that leads to commitment and involvement with the world, and not a turning away from the world. A form of wisdom that I strive for is the ability to know what is needed at a given moment in time. When do I need to reside in that location of stillness and contemplation, and when do I need to get up off my ass and do whatever is needed to be done in terms of physical work, or engagement with others, or confrontation with others? I'm not interested in ranking one type of action over the other.

TWORKOV: Why are so many other people?

HOOKS: I think that it goes back to our relationship with pain. One of the mighty illusions that is constructed in the dailiness of life in our culture is that all pain is a negation of worthiness, that the real chosen people, the real worthy people, are the people that are most free from pain. Don't you think that's true?

TWORKOV: That was a prevalent idea among white Buddhists when Buddhism took off in this culture in the sixties and seventies—that the teachings are about how not to suffer, rather than how best to deal with the inevitable suffering that life deals out.

HOOKS: We see that denial in a lot of New Age thinking in the rhetoric that connects becoming more wealthy, more happy, and more free from all forms of pain with becoming more spiritual.

TWORKOV: Are love and suffering the same?

HOOKS: To be capable of love one has to be capable of suffering and of acknowledging one's suffering. We all suffer, rich and poor. The fact is that when people have material privilege at the enormous expense of others, they live in a state of terror as well. It's the unease of having to protect your gain, which then necessitates even greater control. That's why we see fascism surfacing right now in Europe and the U.S., a compulsion to control. This phrase "New World Order" is so significant because it confirms everybody's sense that life is out of control. And we are weakened by nihilism.

TWORKOV: That's what Cornel West writes about.

HOOKS: Yes. Nihilism is a kind of disease that grips the mind and then grips people in fundamental ways, and can only be subverted by seizing the power that exists in chaos.

TWORKOV: The power of self-agency?

HOOKS: Absolutely. And collective agency, too, because of the idea—as in Nhat Hanh's work—that the self necessarily survives through linkage with the collective community.

TWORKOV: A lot of oppressed people seem to prefer to blame, rather than to relate to the teachings of mind and transformation of consciousness. Your work does not typify either the Black or the female voice in America.

HOOKS: But a lot of the young rap artists are saying the same thing, in a different way. I think KRS-One and the Disposable Heroes of Hiphoprisy are trying to say, "We really are people of the mind," that Black youth are not just creatures of the body. In a lot of contemporary music one hears a certain sense of anguish that is felt in the mind. Malcolm X is such a hero to certain rap musicians because he was totally focused on the mind. Black youth culture is very much aware of that but they are not sure where to go with it.

TWORKOV: For all of your commitments to an integrated view, are there places of conflict between the political and spiritual? As a woman, as an African American?

HOOKS: Absolutely. The places of conflict are always there. Look at this whole question of sexual harassment and sexual violation. What's so interesting is how much it conforms to very traditional notions of gender. In Buddhist practice, intimacy with the teacher is the space of potential violation.

TWORKOV: In your own experience?

HOOKS: In one of my earliest encounters with a Buddhist guide, he tried to have sex with me. I was infinitely more interested in what he had to say about Buddhism than I was in his body. Yet he was saying that the closer I got to his body, the closer I got to what he thought about Buddhism. This is fundamentally discouraging.

Thich Nhat Hanh talks about women in a very traditional way. When I read a book like *Shambhala: [The Sacred] Path of the Warrior* (Shambhala Publications, 1984) I ask myself, "Where am I located in this as a woman?" Again, the mother is evoked in the traditional role of nurturer, and separate from the world of warriorship and lineage that is so clearly defined as male.

TWORKOV: Women are particularly susceptible to abuse with regard to the spiritual qualities of surrender and humility. What do we do about that?

HOOKS: That is tied to reshaping Buddhist practice so that one really sees fundamental change. We all have to have a lived practice. For example, if we see a female who is powerful yet humble, we can learn about the kind of humility that is empowering, and about a form of surrender that does not diminish one's agency. But it seems to me that that "me" has to be altered in the very way we structure any kind of practice, any kind of community.

TWORKOV: And whatever problems we encounter in the Buddhist communities must pale in comparison with those in the Black communities?

HOOKS: The collective Black community does not allow women to become leaders in the same way we allowed Malcolm or Martin to spring up and be in a position of leadership. And nobody in the community wants to deal with that fact. There are a lot of women out there who are able to lead, and the problem is that people will not follow them.

TWORKOV: Do you frame this around one central problem?

HOOKS: The central problem for women is that you can't give up the ego and the self if you haven't established a sense of yourself as subject. It seems to me that questions of humility and surrender don't even come in until one has something to give up.

I do think that women like myself have to integrate the processes by which we change, and speak about those processes more. Gloria Steinem, in *Revolution from Within* (Little Brown and Co., 1991), says that in part there are many women now with skills and resources, but if they still feel shaky in the deep inner core of being, they cannot move forward against patriarchy. This goes back to all I've been saying about victimization. A lot of Black people with resources and skills are so convinced inwardly that they lack something, that they cannot move forward.

TWORKOV: Can you tell us something of your own life that reveals how you arrived at your current understanding?

HOOKS: It was a tremendous liberatory moment in my painful childhood, when I thought, I am more than my pain. In the great holocaust literature, particularly the Nazi Holocaust literature, people say, "All around me there was death and evil and slaughter of innocents, but I had to keep some sense of a transcendent world that proclaims we're more than this evil, despite its power." When I'm genuinely victimized by racism in my daily life, I want to be able to name it, to name that it hurts me, to say that I'm victimized by it. But I don't want to see that as all that I am.

TWORKOV: Sartre's two ways to enter the gas chamber: free and not free. Yet, I must admit that when I read your essay on Anita Hill (in *Black Looks*, South End Press, 1992), I was surprised at how hard you came down on her.

HOOKS: Yes, but I never once tried to deny the reality that she was sexually harassed. At the same time, I said she's more than that sexual harassment. She's also a political conservative who has totally allied herself with the white male supremacist patriarchy, just like Clarence Thomas has. She is anti-abortion and was pro-Bork, for example.

TWORKOV: You also call into question her inability to take responsibility for what happened with Thomas.

HOOKS: Even when she came forward, she was still saying

on TV, "Other people urged me to come forth." She was still presenting herself as a passive person, without agency, responding to other people. That bothered me. And I was disturbed that so many women identified with that. What I want to know is, where is her ability to say, "I feel that this man should not have certain forms of power, and I wanted to come forward of my own free will and not because other people urged me to."

TWORKOV: How do you explain Anita Hill's popularity?

HOOKS: I make bumper stickers in my mind. And one of them is, "Everybody loves a woman who is a victim." Would people love Anita Hill had she actually been able to block Clarence Thomas's appointment? Would she then have been perceived as a woman who was too powerful? What actually catapulted her into stardom was the fact that she lost. That even though she came forward, even though she sacrificed a lot, she didn't attain the desired goal. And this is absolutely in tune with the culture of domination. I remember reading a book on lying that said Americans are lying more and more in daily life, with simple things such as how are you feeling today, or what did you do today, who did you talk to on the phone? And I'm thinking, "My god, if people cannot tell the truth about things that have absolutely no layer of risk, of danger, how do we expect people then to stand up in situations of crisis that are matters of life and death?" To the degree, again, that people do not wish to experience pain, they will engage in denial. And denial, I think, is always a practice of narcissism because it's always about protecting the self.

Again, that's why I like Butterfield's piece, because he says that these narratives of victimage go back to the self, and that denial protects what people think has to be protected and guarded.

TWORKOV: And there are also real abuses. How can we deal with that?

HOOKS: What was problematic for me about Butterfield's piece was that I don't think he gave us the whole picture in the sense that he wasn't really willing to acknowledge those real abuses. It's a lot harder to frame your argument if you say, "Yes, exploitation occurs, but something else occurs at the same time. Yes, racism occurs, but something else occurs at the same time." How is one to get in touch with all of those different things?

TWORKOV: But how do you make a distinction when, for example, someone turns to you and says, "You feel victimized? That's your problem." The Zen communities functioned this way for years in response to individual complaints.

HOOKS: People are genuinely exploited, but that reality doesn't take away from the many, many instances where people give up their own agency and, in that way, help create a setting for exploitation. Only by holding on to the sense that we can never be completely dehumanized by "others" can we create a redemptive model. If you're attached to being a victim, there is no hope. One has to work out points of blockage, or victimage to agency, and from there build a collective process that can change an institution and can change a societal direction.

TWORKOV: Let's take a version of that in Buddhism. The gender problems with Thich Nhat Hanh, for example, are not "abuses" but there's an attitude. Do you "confront" the teacher?

HOOKS: If there was more of a collective call on the part of students to say to a teacher, "We are concerned that there are all these other areas that we see changes and growth in your thought, but when it comes to questions of gender and family, we don't." I think a real problem is how we frame devotion to the teacher. And the question of questioning. That's something that has to be done more collectively. I think that if an individual alone tries to question, they get crushed, sometimes not just by the teacher, but by other students.

TWORKOV: What is the dynamic of victimization in our society?

HOOKS: A culture of domination like ours says to people: there is nothing in you that is of value, everything of value is outside you and must be acquired. The tremendous message in this culture is one of devaluation. Low self-esteem is a national epidemic and victimization is the flip side of domination.

TWORKOV: To what extent is your work considered a contradiction by progressive Blacks?

HOOKS: Not that much. Because people hear me saying revolution must begin with the self, but it has to be united with some kind of social vision.

But I see many people deeply engaged in complicity with the very structures of domination they critique. And I think that that is an illusion. It's true that often, let's say, when I talk about theory, I do have to argue for the fact that theory making or certain forms of critical thinking are essential to a process of change because people have been led to believe you can have change without contemplation.

To a lot of people they would say, "You can use your rage." I feel that, yes, I can use my rage, but only if there's something else there with that rage.

TWORKOV: Take the Rodney King case. The verdict comes down, the cops are not guilty. How do you go from there to not feeling victimized?

HOOKS: I don't think it's that you don't feel victimized. You acknowledge that you're being victimized. But the question becomes, is rage the only or the most appropriate response? What would people have thought if rather than Black people exploding in rage about the Rodney King incident, if there had been a week of silence? Something that would have just so unsettled people's stereotypes about Black people.

TWORKOV: One of the things that characterized the riots was the tremendous empathy across the country for King.

HOOKS: The sad thing is that the empathy came from a sense of total victimization.

TWORKOV: So they are victimized but they have self-agency.

HOOKS: Right. I think it serves the interest of domination if the only way people can respond to victimage is rage. Because then they really are just mirroring the very conditions that brought them into victimization. Violence. The conquering of other people's territory. If we talk about the burning down of other people's property as a takeover, is that different from what the U.S. did in Grenada or Iraq? It's not a stepping outside of the program, it's a mirroring back, and that's why I think so many white people and masses of other groups felt sympathy. Because the other side of total victimage is rage.

TWORKOV: Victimage . . .

HOOKS: I was thinking about the victim identity. If you look at the early feminist movement and the women who were seeing themselves the most as complete victims also had this blind rage, because those two things go together. That's why it's so dangerous, because then you're not operating outside the forces of domination at all. You're still tied intimately to that psychology of domination.

TWORKOV: So consciousness is the only way to transmute the forces of domination.

HOOKS: The only way. There is no change without contemplation. The whole image of Buddha under the Bodhi tree says here is an action taking place that may not *appear* to be a meaningful action.

BELL HOOKS BY LAWRENCE CHUA

INTERVIEW BY LAWRENCE CHUA
BOMB MAGAZINE
JULY 1,1994

Love takes us to places we might not ordinarily go. Ask anyone who's engaged the work of bell hooks. Her fearless inquiries and passionate provocations have left us questioning the once familiar terrain of cultural identity while simultaneously affirming the complexity of our own lived experiences. In her many books of critical writing, including *Black Looks, Yearning, Breaking Bread: Insurgent Black Intellectual Life*, (with Cornel West) and the forthcoming *Outlaw Culture*; her self-help book, *Sisters of the Yam*; her recent collection of poetry, *A Woman's Mourning Song*, her artistic collaborations and her many public presentations, hooks has hit raw nerves, delving into the possibilities of culture as a place of resistance to white supremacy, capitalism and patriarchy. While most critical theorists speak about popular culture from the lofty perches of the academy, hooks has always insinuated herself in the fray.

This interview with one of America's most indispensable and independent thinkers initiates a new series in *BOMB* devoted to the ideas of today's most influential theorists.

LAWRENCE CHUA: Recently, you were at a conference on Black cinema where Stanley Crouch suggested that artists like Snoop Doggy Dog should be exterminated. How did you respond?

BELL HOOKS: While it's crucial to critique the sexism and the misogyny of rappers like Snoop Doggy Dog, it is essential for everyone to remember that they are not only more complex than the way they represent themselves, they're more complex than the way white society represents them as well. This notion, that Snoop Doggy Dog defines himself "as he really is" is something I reject. He clearly defines himself with a persona that works in cultural production in this society. The most discouraging aspect of that conference for me was this insistence on liberal individualism, as though people's acts are disconnected from larger structures and larger forces of representation. Even Stanley Crouch wasn't responding to my points. He was actually playing to those larger, mainstream cultural forces that reward him for saying really negative things about rap. I don't believe it when people like Stanley Crouch say they are really concerned about misogyny. One can certainly read his essay on Toni Morrison and see incredible examples of virulent sexism and misogyny. I saw a continuum between the violence of a Snoop Doggy Dog and the violence of a Stanley Crouch, and I didn't really see them as being separate and distinct entities. At the conference, I confessed that I have really violent impulses that sometimes listening to some panels I had wanted to come out and shoot people. The audience laughed, but I wasn't being funny, and I wasn't saying it to be cute or exhibitionist. I was acknowledging that the violent impulses don't just exist out there in Black youth or in the underclass, but that they reside in people like myself as well—people who have our PhDs and our good jobs. But that doesn't mean that my life is not tormented by rageful or irrational, violent impulses. It does mean that instead of shooting people, I go home and write a critique. My irrational impulse to want to kill people who bore me or whose ideas are not very complex, clearly has to do with an exaggerated response to situations where I feel powerless. I think Black people, across class, have many moments in our lives when we feel utterly powerless to change the direction of situations. And we don't deal with this collectively, because we're so in denial about it. It is significant that the urge to exterminate was aroused by a moral standpoint wherein vulgarity must be dissed. This has a lot to do with censorship. I'm not talking about mainstream censorship. I'm talking about groups that claim to have progressive agendas, but also have practices of censorship, that involve their wanting to check people around crossing boundaries that "don't make our movement look good." There is a whole way of structuring conferences so that they end up being these celebratory events where a certain censorship takes place in the interest of maintaining unity. I see that as part of the colonizing mentality that says, "In case white people are looking, we need to present ourselves as this unified nation so we can't have these all-out dialectical exchanges where we show our differences." We need multiple voices that mirror our multiple subjectivities. There's a cognitive dissonance between what is really being said by cultural critics—we're into border crossing, and cultural hybridity—and yet, when we come together, we still mirror the model of a unitary voice.

CHUA: How is your own work challenging those boundaries? When we had lunch a few months ago, you were about to go on a TV talk show. You said you were doing this because you weren't reaching the audience you needed to start reaching.

HOOKS: I went on the *Ricki Lake* show and it was a disaster. But it was a great experience. There are academics who do work on popular culture, but who really just do a lot of theoretical talking about popular culture and don't actually enter those spaces that are much more full of contradictions, hostilities, and tensions. I heard those Black folks in the audience at the *Ricki Lake* show saying, "We don't agree with Doctor hooks. We're not even going to call her 'Doctor.' She doesn't even know what she's talking about." I felt seriously assaulted, but at the same time, this was a different rage experience than sitting at home writing my cool article on the discourse of talk shows. To actually go there, and to participate, and see, and walk off the TV set because the politics of what was happening there were very disturbing to me . . . They had told us that there would be a "special guest" but they hadn't said that it would be this Nazi woman. But I wanted to go on that show because *Ricki Lake* has an incredible number of Black viewers between the ages of sixteen and twenty-five, and those are exactly the people who are not in women's studies classes, or in cool cultural studies classes where they're learning about a Cornel West or a bell hooks. I used a quote by Snoop Doggy Dog at the NYU conference on Black cinema, that really meant a lot to me. He said, "I don't rap. I just talk. I want to be able to relax and conversate with my people." Are we, cultural workers situated in the academy, developing a jargon about cultural production that does not allow us to "conversate and cross" these very borders that we're talking about how cool it would be to cross? If we don't find a way to "conversate," all we're ever talking about is that those of us who have certain forms of class privilege can enter the low-down and dirty spaces and take what we want to get out of those spaces, and take our asses right back home. That is really crucial for the future of cultural criticism in the United States, for the future of magazines like *BOMB*, and the other kinds of magazines that many of us enjoy, *Vibe*, *Details*. How much are we conversating?

CHUA: How does your own work accommodate that kind of conversating?

HOOKS: I am willing to debase myself in whichever way possible, and be treated like shit as I was on the *Ricki Lake* show. We can't minimize that because it's a very different experience from lecturing at places like Yale and Harvard where crowds of people are bowing down and saying, "We're not worthy, we're not worthy," than to be among a whole crowd of young people waiting to get in to this show and talk, who could give a fuck about bell hooks. Or to be in Flint, Michigan, talking to a hundred fifth graders, who have no idea what I'm about, and to have to come up with a language that can cross those borders effectively. The point is not just to be some sort of sterile role model who stands up and gives a canned talk. One of the things that I've been critiqued a lot about is the level of confession in my work and my public "performances." If you read my early work, there's very little attention to the details of my life, very little personal stuff. One of the things that I found, as I tried to cross boundaries, was that I had to give people something that allowed them to identify with what I was saying, and not just offer some abstract idea that might not have any relevance to their lives. That is all about the function of story. When those little fifth graders had question and answer, the first thing they wanted to know was, "How much money do you make?" Now, these fifth graders are coming out of one of the most economically depressed states in this country. Most of their parents work in the auto industry. How much money you make is more crucial to them than the relationship between feminism and Marxism. But to answer that question honestly and openly can be a way to then talk about feminism and the structure of capitalism. In fact, we went from how much money I made to, "Did you guys know how much on the average women make?" People were really shocked, because they so believe in the myth of democracy, they all thought women receive equal pay for equal work. Crossing borders means that at times I share things that I don't want to share. But if you really see yourself as a worker for freedom, then the challenge is also on you to sacrifice whatever notions of privacy that many of us would want to hold onto, especially if we are clinging to bourgeois models of self and identity. These fifth graders wanted to understand book production, because I know that they have parents who are saying, "You don't want to be a writer, writers don't make anything. If you work in the plant this is what is available to you." Class is the most uncool topic in cultural studies in the United States. It's easier to look at the Black identity of the Hughes Brothers who made *Menace II Society*, than to acknowledge the class positionality of these young men and to talk about how it may have shaped their opinion. Maybe they find a gangsta in the hood really glamorous because it's not the world that they emerged from. That's a class critique that gets submerged under an evocation of racial solidarity, or racial intervention. These young Black men are intervening in the Hollywood apparatus in some ways by their very presence, by the racial images they create. Whereas, if we look at class, we don't see intervention in Hollywood. We actually see a reproduction of a certain relation to the working class and the poor. Hollywood has always had visions of the working class and the poor, cross race, created by people who often are mired in contempt and fantasy, and/or voyeuristic fantasy about what those class realities are really like.

CHUA: Your last book, *Sisters of the Yam*, speaks to and across many of those class borders. It was conceived of as a self-help book. How difficult was it to write a book that was not going to be sold as an academic text?

HOOKS: It was exciting for me to write *Sisters of the Yam* and try to find a more vernacular way to talk about certain things. It's also exciting to get a response from that. People would be shocked by the number of everyday people who take the time to write me a letter about a book. It wouldn't matter what kind of books I was writing, if I didn't get the feedback from communities of readers who let me know that the books are actually working. That fills me with a certain kind of joy. To think of certain ways of writing as activism is crucial. What does it matter if we write eloquently about decolonization if it's just white privileged kids reading our eloquent theory about it? Masses of Black people suffer from internalized racism, our intellectual work will never impact on their lives if we do not move it out of the academy. That's why I think mass media is so important. Popular magazines and television have to be seen as central vehicles for the dissemination of intellectual thought. We are looking at a culture where millions of people don't read or write. If I want to get the message out there I have to use some other format. I do a lot more radio than I would like to do because it still has a place in the lives of many working-class people in our society. It amazes me.

CHUA: There are some obvious limitations to personalizing theoretical writing. How do you debate the theoretical element of a sentence that begins with, "As a twenty-seven-year-old Malaysian house queen" without taking on the identity of the person who is saying it?

HOOKS: Since we live in a cultural climate, especially in the academy where the realm of the personal is devalued, when you use that standpoint it may lead listeners to mishear. That voice may be very complex but people actually may not hear the complexity. I gave this talk framed around the idea of "love takes me to places I would ordinarily not go." I raised the whole question of love in a very psychoanalytical way, framing the discussion around notions of recognition and mirroring. I was really sad when so many people came up to me to say, "We love you," because they'd missed the point. When you are a woman and you use a confessional narrative, people tend to think there is not some more complex structure of thinking or philosophy behind that narrative. I needed to bring some of that background thinking more to the fore, otherwise, it failed. But even if it failed to do as much as I wanted it to, it does not devalue the courage of trying to bring the voice of lived experience and confessional witnessing into our intellectual processing in a way that does not reduplicate that whole pattern of estrangement from self and ideas. I am passionate about ideas. They're not just the stuff of spectatorship and entertainment to me. They're a life-blood, and that's what makes the intellectual process so radically different from the academic process. Part of the challenge for insurgent intellectuals, particularly those of us who are artists in this society, is to pull back from academe, actually, and academic settings, precisely to break this notion that has become so popular in the culture, that the two experiences are one.

CHUA: I was curious how your own critical language is developing, with that strategy in mind.

HOOKS: I've been trying to use different languages for different settings, and it's hard. One of the things I'm trying to do is break with the traditional essay format, which has been an exhilarating and exciting format for me. But it also takes time. I'd like to do work that is more mixed media and pastiche. But when you want to make a shift, then you come up against an industry that doesn't want you to because they've already got a proven product. This has been very harmful to African American writers in general. I am constantly working to shift my voice and to try to use it differently. In my poetry writing, for example, I use a voice that tends to be much more abstract than the voice of my writing. A lot of people, when I first tried to get my poems published, said, "There's nothing Black about these poems." Damn, how often do you have to prove that you're Black? It's not enough that I'm a Black woman writing these poems, but there has to be something in the language that tips off the reader, that you are reading something by a Black woman writer. There's this constant struggle to actually have a lived practice that really mirrors this theoretical bullshit about hybridity and polyphonic voices. I've always cursed like a sailor. I learned how to curse from my grandmother. I've always had a certain kind of street language that has been essential to how I've defined myself. But, it's a language that I keep under wraps. In certain settings, you can let that language out, but if you let it out in this other setting, you'll get checked immediately. I'm putting a lot of pressure on myself to "come out of the closet"—that great metaphor for everything these days, in the sense of trying to speak certain languages in locations where I didn't speak them because I tried to conform to the dictates of those locations. What is border crossing, if in every setting, you simply scan the place and figure out the appropriate rules and abide by them. That ends up sounding much more like social fascism than any rigorous transgression.

CHUA: In *Yearning*, that "street language" is often set apart from your theorizing by quotation marks, while in *Black Looks* and *Sisters of the Yam* it's a more organic component of the syntax. Have editors become more receptive to that linguistic transgression?

HOOKS: I went through this period where I would try to use more street language and it would all come back to me, completely edited back to standard English. These few months that I've been living in New York, I've really been overwhelmed by the degree to which there is no racial integration in publishing in our society. I'm awed by the lack, not just of the concrete visible presence of people of color, but also the failure to have progressive white people. We should be able to have spaces in this society where people of color are not present, but where anti-racist perspectives will inform how things are organized and what takes place. No wonder the wheel has to be invented again, and again, and again. We're being told by the publishing world that our major buying audience is a white audience. The presumption is of an unenlightened white audience, and when everything you write should be pitched to that audience, it becomes a really troubling question of what voice you use, and what space you can occupy. We're not just talking about the straight publishing world, we're talking about those vehicles in our culture that claim to represent some kind of alternative. That says that we have a lot of work to do to truly create a culture of resistance, that's not just occupied by people of color individually knocking on the door for change, but that's really occupied by lots of people who see the necessity for having a more complex intellectual artistic life in this culture.

CHUA: Debates around representation have focused almost exclusively on who is in the frame, as if it were separate from how the narrative unfolds. That's made it difficult for Black writers whose work refuses that separation between truth and beauty to publish.

HOOKS: If your perspective isn't "I'm negating blackness, in the interest of writing more experimentally," but, "I'm affirming blackness and I still want to write experimentally," that's when you have trouble selling your product. The question I'm asked most often about my writing is: Who is the perceived audience? There's this sense that if you really want to have that crossover audience, you've got to simplify, you've got to translate, you've got to make everything clear. But we know that there are a lot of interesting books by white writers that don't simplify, that don't make everything clear, and people presume that they will have an audience. There's a myth about artistic freedom, that it resides with the individual writer, and not that artistic freedom has to be mirrored in the publishing practices of a culture, or when you're talking about art, the practices of galleries and museums. It cannot be something that becomes a cultural norm simply by individual artists insisting that their work is an expression of artistic freedom. Even though so many of us can name white supremacy, we go on to express shock and naive surprise that things are done the way they are or that our views aren't represented. To some extent, one's views do have an opportunity of being represented if you dare to put forth some of the labor. I feel like I labor for things. A lot of times it is a sacrifice. I have this deep feeling that the meaning of sacrifice has been really lost in this culture. When I look back at the civil rights struggle, I am awed by people's willingness to sacrifice personal comfort and well-being to make some changes. What's sad is that significance of sacrifice seems to be solely embedded in religion in our society, because religion has not had the force for young people that it had twenty years ago in many of our lives. Look at Malcolm X. Everyone who is pimping him for their own opportunistic gains doesn't talk about the fact that this man lived in relative poverty as he tried to spread his mission. How many of us are committed to living on the edge in that way? I'm certainly not. I'm working hard not to have to live that way, even as I want to hold to the principle of sacrifice and be ready when the moment comes to do what needs to be done to end domination.

CHUA: As you said, the idea of sacrifice is so caught up in religious belief, there is a tendency to oversimplify it. How do you strategize something like sacrifice?

HOOKS: Part of why so many of us came out of radical '60s politics and jumped into Eastern religion was because, more than Christianity, it evoked a balance. How do you balance that commitment to social change where you don't just burn out and give yourself over to an almost negative ethic of sacrifice? How do you create inner harmony and balance that allows you to sacrifice when necessary and to withhold when necessary? I can remember how deeply affected I was by the Buddhist nun in Vietnam who set herself on fire in the interest of protesting the war. How far do we go and what do we give? I still find religion to be the place that tempers my spirit. A friend and I have battled around the whole question: "Are there other locations where these values of moral discipline, integrity and sacrifice can be taught?" We can teach those ethics to young children without teaching them religion, but it's hard to know how to bring an ethical dimension into political work and artistic practice in a culture that is so obscenely hedonistic. That's why people like me might not fall back on organized religion but fall back on the construction of more private spiritual practice that enables us to think about issues like sacrifice and service. Growing up, we were taught to believe we existed to service the cause of racial uplift and ending white supremacy. The young Blacks that I teach today are into that kind of liberalism that says, "I'm mainly here to service myself first and if I want to join some radical cause I can." For many years I wouldn't have been able to even think of improving myself without heightening the freedom and well-being of my community. It really was entering white institutions of higher learning that disrupted that vision of living to serve the community and the cause of racial uplift. Where is liberal individualism most taught, but in academic institutions? They exist to produce the privileged classes. To make them come into being it's very important to have people repudiate any ethic of communalism in favor of privatized thinking.

CHUA: I wonder how much of that ethic of communalism comes from being part of a rural, or even a suburban, community. Do you think your rural background has informed a lot of your critical practice?

HOOKS: Kentucky is one of the states that is very feudal in a lot of ways. Coming from there carries some of the really negative aspects of a feudal culture, but it also was a world that really did believe in certain kinds of values. The poor are consistently represented in this culture's mass media as having no values or ethics, yet where I grew up there was no correlation between poverty and lack of integrity. Poor back-woods Kentucky folk, my people had a relationship to loyalty and honor, a whole ethical dimension that was completely divorced from materiality. I find it amazing that across race and class, we live in a country that's very determined by geographic location. We have very few voices that come to us from rural experience in America. The educated people from those regions actually learn to translate away from our vernacular cultures in the interest of getting some play and consideration in the larger public world. I was talking to my dad, who's in his mid-seventies and is doing poorly. He was going on about how he worked for thirty-some years and was never absent from his job. One of the things that I tell my dad all the time is that the discipline I have as a writer is not anything that I learned at Stanford University. I got it from this working-class background where disciplined work was really valued. My dad kept using the phrase "marvelously blessed." To think that a Black man working in the South at a "menial job" would reflect back on that experience and declare that he feels marvelously blessed that he was not absent from his job in thirty-some years . . . I was touched. He was speaking in the vernacular of our region and I thought about how much I'd lost that capacity because I'm not there enough. There is a beauty to vernacular speech and culture in America. Mass media is one of the forces that aggressively works to wipe out that cultural and regional specificity.

CHUA: When I came in this afternoon, we were talking about the differences between Black British thought and Black American thought. How do you think these issues are played out across the Atlantic? Why has Black Britain been able to produce the kind of radical cultural work and theory that we here in America haven't?

HOOKS: Because the material rewards are not there in British culture, there's less of a temptation to sell out in the same way. I'm not acting like I think Black British people have some kind of integrity that is different. But the integrity is challenged here by the existence of a structure of reward. I feel more linked to Black British thinkers right now, because a lot of the choices that I make in what I write and how I write it actually prevent me from reaping those rewards. I'm still struggling both politically, morally, and ethically to be an independent thinker. There is this fear of radical openness that's making Black social and critical thought infinitely more homogeneous than we should ever want it to be. Why do we have to be threatened by the notion of a different voice or a dissenting voice? I feel this a lot lately around issues of censorship and what I want to be able to talk about in the future. I really want to write in a complex way about Black sexuality and I feel that there's tremendous resistance to a discussion of Black sexuality that does not reproduce certain norms. In terms of representation, we are perhaps portrayed as the most oversexed group in this society. How has that affected our actual sex lives? Do we exist in a culture where nothing that we can do sexually is equal to the hype? We have uncovered work that suggests Martin Luther King fucked all the time, but we can't find one article that would talk about what the place of sexuality was in his life. To what extent did the enormous sacrifices that he made as a public persona influence his compulsive sexual behavior? Did we see any public discourse about whether Malcolm X had or did not have homosexual relations? If this is our shining Black prince, our manhood, does this open up the possibility for a revolution in how we think about Black masculinity? Nor do we have a lot of complex writing about Black resistance to racism and our simultaneous embrace of American national identity, which we clearly saw exposed during the Gulf War. I think the issues of nationhood are much more central to Black folk in Europe because they are minorities in the countries that they live in and they haven't had the legacies of resistance that we have here. When people evoke Martin Luther King's "I Have a Dream," they completely erase that radical critique that is present in sermons and speeches like "A Testament of Hope," wherein he suggests we must move beyond a national identity to a profound critique of imperialism and global militarism. That's the Martin Luther King that will not be taught to every little schoolkid.

CHUA: You've often juxtaposed the trope of nation and family with the more fluid notion of community.

HOOKS: It suggests something that can be made and remade wherever you might be. Communities of resistance suggest something that has to be explained, while nation and family already conjure up specific kinds of images and forms of bonding for people. There's a tremendous mounting fascism in this culture and it's very scary to see it finding such presence in expression of African American life. Basically the educated body of Black people who are cultural workers, writers, artists, musicians, etc. tend to be deeply invested in bourgeois values on all levels. People evoke jazz as expressive of these far-reaching radical oppositions to norms, but they really haven't been carried over in habits of daily life. Those very jazz musicians, particularly the men who were so groundbreaking in their musical crossing of boundaries, tended to be very narrow in their thinking about gender and patriarchy. Miles Davis is such a good example of that because he vocalized his reactionary perspectives on gender. No one talks about the fact that in all these cases of sexual aggression with Black public figures, like Tupac Shakur, the woman has been Black. The cultural response would be very different to these events if the women were white. Black men do victimize Black women but that victimization is coded as a response to racism, and not as, let's talk about racism and what Black men get from patriarchy. What do Black men get through this rhetoric of nation, in terms of their power in domestic space? That's not a discourse that white culture is fascinated with, because they don't give a fuck about what happens in Black domestic space.

CHUA: You've talked about how figures like Tupac Shakur and Ice Cube disrupt essential notions of Black masculinity. Your understanding of gangsta rap is very different from the dominant feminist line.

HOOKS: People presume that because I'm a feminist thinker they know I'm gonna trash rap, especially gangsta rap. I can challenge the sexism and misogyny of it, but I can embrace the rage that is implicit in it and the sense of powerlessness that undergirds it. It is such a challenge to be able to see that you can not identify with something about individuals and still have parts of them that you might embrace and engage. When I interviewed Ice Cube, he was insisting on the power of the Black father in the home. I was yelling, "Are you really trying to tell me that if you have unloving Black fathers in the home, we're going to have a generation of healthy kids?" Finally he acknowledged that just having a father present who's not caring is really not going to produce some healthy children. That's the kind of exchange that we should be trying to bring to the floor and not these simplistic representations of sexism and misogyny. It's so hard because these men both disrupt and reinscribe at the same time. One has to be vigilant in your response but that means you have to be engaged and I think that so much cultural criticism is nonparticipatory. The cultural critic stands so much at a distance from what he or she writes about. That distance is always dangerous in that it has the possibility of reinscribing the status quo, co-opting and appropriating in the interest of making the status quo appear more chic, more open than it finally ever really is.

CHUA: I wonder also how you see the function of groups like The Disposable Heroes of Hiphoprisy, whose work on very obvious levels challenges that kind of status quo, and yet has been met with so much resistance in terms of the marketplace.

HOOKS: I follow their work and like it and other groups like Arrested Development. I interviewed Speech from Arrested Development and I talked to a lot of young Black women about him. They said, "Yeah, but after a while their music is just boring." Then I think we do get into the tension around notions of funkiness and getting down and being down. I think a perpetual tension for any of us who engage in any kind of revolutionary political visions of transformation is how do we keep the funk? We never talk about what if people aren't drawn by the sexism and the misogyny, but are instead drawn by a sense of recklessness, a willingness to transcend limits and to call out shit graphically. Yet we in our progressive visions don't account for those yearnings to be on the edge. I felt that lust when I was young and I feel it now. How can we have some models of radicalism that also incorporate what it is to transgress in a manner that is expressive, colorful, exciting, and even dangerous? What allows me to hold to whatever sweetness I may find in a word like "bitch," that doesn't translate into some subjugation of women? One of the things that I believe is that this kind of theory cannot be done in the same old privatized way. It has to emerge from collaborative exchange, from border crossing of an Ice Cube and a bell hooks trying to jam it out together and jamming one another. Or for me saying to Cornel West, "I'm sorry Cornel, young Black men are not going to say, 'Gee, I really want to look like that guy in those three-piece suits.'" [*laughter*] That's not saying that we shouldn't be able to embrace those suits as some sign of cool, but the fact is they are no sign of cool to the young and hip who want to be down! They're not even a sign of cool for me. When I broached this on stage with Cornel, he seemed to be put off by the question and so was the audience. I was not embracing a rhetoric that suggested Black kids should be looking at the man in the suit and not the man in the leather coat as cool, as a role model. I was suggesting that the man in the suit might need to change to hold our interest—to capture our imagination. The spirit of transgression that is so central to both my intellectual practice and my political practice is much more tied in with what people like Queen Latifah and Ice T are saying than with what other academics are saying. These are exciting times. I have this deep belief in destiny, so I'm trying to live with what is my destiny here in New York. This is the last place on earth that I would ever have imagined myself living. I feel driven here by forces beyond my control. But I am excited to see whether I can, in conjunction and collaboration with other people, have New York City be more a place where some of transgressively radical open critical thought and artistic production can emerge. That kind of truly avant-garde revolutionary cultural production will not happen if we don't begin to theorize it into existence as well, if we can't see that theory can be a catalyst for artistic practice and vice versa. It is that mutual interplay that might bring the element of risk and sacrifice back into our artistic and cultural practice.

TENDER HOOKS

INTERVIEW BY LISA JERVIS
BITCH MAGAZINE
WINTER 2000

Though bell hooks may be one of feminism's sharpest thinkers and fiercest critics of white supremacist capitalist patriarchy (a phrase that pops up often in her work), her favorite
topic these days, in conversation and in writing, is love. Last
winter's *All About Love* explored romantic love, spiritual love,
family love, and most of all profoundly politicized love. Next
winter's *Salvation: Black People in Love* will no doubt pick up
where *All About Love* left off (and following that will come
her second children's book, *Homemade Love*). Not that the
incredibly prolific hooks would stop there, she continues to
add to her list of classic feminist texts at a brisk pace. One
of her two books out this fall is *Feminism Is for Everybody*, a
primer on feminism that, with chapter headings like "Liber-
ating Marriage and Partnership" and "Total Bliss," often reads
more like a wish list of fertile feminist possibility. We caught
up with her by phone to talk about self-help books, the penis,
Nurse Betty—and, of course, the thoughts of love that have
brought a different kind of passion to her work.

LISA JERVIS: In *Feminism Is for Everybody*, you write, "If
women and men want to know love we have to yearn for
feminism." Can you talk about this connection between love
and feminism?

BELL HOOKS: I keep telling people that I'm going to be the high priestess of love for the next few years, and so many people keep saying, "Oh, well, bell hooks is turning soft 'cause she's focusing on love." And I think, Oh, no, not the love I'm talking about—because I'm really talking about a love that's grounded in a vision of mutuality and communion and sharing; to me that is so deeply related to feminism because I feel like as long as we have gender inequality and inequity and sexism and patriarchy, we can't have mutuality. What we have is a constant paradigm of domination, a constant sense that in the world there's always a top and bottom in our relationships, there's always a subordinated person and a person who is dominant.

One thing that l have felt strongly over the years is that while I have seen relationships between heterosexual men and women change a lot, what I often see is that if the man assumes a more nurturing, more emotional and giving position, the woman is often cold and aloof and ungiving. We certainly see this in a lot of movies—even in a movie like *High Fidelity*, which l really enjoyed, we still see that you have a certain kind of warmth posited with the man and a coldness in the energy of the so-called New Woman, the young, professional career woman. It seems to me that this is still within the same old paradigm of every relationship [having] a submissive party and a dominant party. It's just that people are more comfortable now with men taking on the submissive roles, but that's not what feminist visions of true love are about, because those visions are about mutuality. They're about a world where we can both be self-actualized in a relationship, whether it's two men together or two women together or two transgendered people or whatever our arrangements. Mutuality is at the heart of this vision of a more politicized understanding of love as a force that transforms domination.

JERVIS: How can we put that into practice in our lives and in our relationships?

HOOKS: There has to be a lot more conversation and communication than people often have in relationships. As someone who's been in alternative heterosexual relationships often in my life—very, very carefully throughout relationships—what I can testify is that you have a lot more discussion in those relationships. My ex-boyfriend, to whom I dedicated *All About Love* and to whom my new book *Salvation* is dedicated, is a younger guy who is very quiet compared to me, and not as analytically motivated as I am. One of the things we did, by his suggestion, was have these little weekly meetings for 20 minutes—because I tend to talk so much more than he and it's the sort of structure that allowed him a space to have an equal voice, so to speak.

JERVIS: And that's really groundbreaking. Most people think planning like that takes the spontaneity out of it.

HOOKS: He came out of a counseling background; he was working with Emerge, which is an organization that deals with men who batter. So he had a hyperconsciousness about the whole need to process in a different kind of way. Ten years later, we continue to have these conversations, and he feels that I often don't abide by the time frame that we set up.

Recently, I read again *Men Are from Mars, Women Are from Venus*. I was so struck by how that book doesn't even entertain the possibility of mutuality, and what it does is offer a real paradigm for people to stay within their very sexist-designed gender roles but get along with one another. That's why I think it's been so powerful.

JERVIS: Because it makes people feel comfortable to stay with that?

HOOKS: No, because people are unhappy, honey. [Laughs.] People are tired of fighting, people are tired of living in misery. I think it's so popular because it offers people something that feminist theory, no matter how radical and visionary, tends not to offer people, which is a vision of what you can do to bring peace. And I think that people really want to have more peace in our relationships and in our daily lives. Many of us have come from dysfunctional families where there's been lots of conflict and strife. So I think that's part of the popularity of that book—it's a model of healing, but it's pro-patriarchal, so it is not threatening to men. I think here it's really important to say benevolent patriarchy—because obviously John Gray's book and a lot of other books by New Age men are not pro a more abusive, coercive patriarchy. But benevolent patriarchy is still a vision that says that at the end of the day, men's needs and values and longings matter more.

Let's say you're a feminist woman in a relationship with a really sexist guy who never talks. Every time you try to get that person to talk, you suffer, and then suddenly you have a book that says, "Don't try to talk to him when he's in his cave, just accept his being quiet." It's sort of like saying, "Don't try to demand of this person emotional growth and that they not be an adolescent." It's like saying, "Accept him as a person who is emotionally underdeveloped," whereas a model of mutuality might suggest that both people need to go and talk about how they can emotionally develop together—as opposed to saying, "Well, just accept that he doesn't want to do this."

JERVIS: To me there's something about that model of looking at things that very much naturalizes gender roles—it says that this is the way men *are* and this is the way women *are*.

HOOKS: When I go out into the high schools or just into an everyday world talking about feminism, the people from 6 to 25, that's exactly what they bring up. That's exactly their wall of resistance. I don't even have difficulty with us saying that there's some kind of hardcore biological determinism, because what we really know is that everything can be changed through socialization. So even if you want to say we start off in some kind of binary that is oppositional, it can be altered at birth. So let's talk about why people have such resistance to altering that—[people] who believe in some kind of fixed biological destiny—since we're quite willing to alter all other kinds of destinies. Sometimes when I think of the incredible revolution people have made with technology, moving from being fearful of technology to people of all classes in our nation believing everybody should know how to use a computer…we know that people can make incredible leaps away from anything that we call natural or biologically determined.

And I find it interesting that whenever we're talking about gender equality, people want to fix biology in some kind of absolute unchanging space rather than say, Nothing has been altered more in the scientific revolutions of modernity than this thing we might call biology.

JERVIS: It's like when people say, "Oh, well, all men cheat because they need to spread their seed and it goes back to when we were in the caves." Okay, but we're not in the caves anymore.

HOOKS: Exactly. If those hungry men in the caves were ever even thinking about cheating. They were probably thinking much more about, *How am I gonna get some food?* And I think that even when we try to have those kinds of symbolic things about archaic society, people don't even have a realistic sense that, hey, back then food was really hard to come by. So much emphasis on sexual desire is very Western: If we think globally, masses of people in the world spend the day just trying to get some water to drink and enough food to make it through the day. The idea that everything is related to and revolves around sex is completely part of our Western sensibility. And I'm not downgrading that, but I think we should own that as peculiar and unique to advanced capitalist worlds that we have leisure. I'm always struck when I'm in the desert somewhere in Africa that people don't have time to sit around all day thinking about who they're going to fuck. And we can frequently sit around thinking all day about who we're going to fuck.

I'm writing a new book, slowly, about space and making space, and the whole question of privacy in the world and who has space. Even the way we think about sex and gendered arrangements in the West is so tied to our notion that everybody has this space. If you even take the concept of John Gray's—"if he needs to go off and be in his cave"—the fact is, in countries where you've got 10 people living in 400 square feet, nobody gets to go off and be in any kind of cave that's not symbolic.

Part of creating a liberatory eroticism that is feminist, that is maximizing of everyone's well-being, is to think globally about different ways of living in the world and to be mindful of the fact that so much of the way we live in the world—like the idea that you get to get in your bed at night by yourself or with one other person of your choice—[is very different from] how masses of people in the world are sleeping, which is, guess what, with lots of other people around.

JERVIS: What do you think are the most pressing issues for feminism right now?

HOOKS: To me the most pressing issues for feminism remain the same as 10 or 20 years ago. One is to have a renewed feminist movement that starts with a vision that feminism is not just for women. That's one of the reasons I called my new book *Feminism Is for Everybody*, because so much of how our traditional radical and revolutionary feminism was structured was with the idea that feminism was really about women, and not a politic that was about everybody—about ending sexism and sexist domination and oppression, which is a definition that I think is so simple and useful because it says that the target may not be men, it has to be all of us. The other day I was saying to this guy, "I hate men who wear jewelry." This is a sexism within myself that I am still dealing with, that somehow jewelry on men tends to turn me off, and that after all my own evolution as a feminist thinker I still find spaces in myself where I see a kind of old notion of who should be doing what.

I think that there's just so much education for critical consciousness for everybody that feminism did not do. Where are our television commercials? Where are our billboards? Where are feminist marketing firms that are going out into the world saying to people: This is how your product could reflect more clearly gender equality or gender justice. I don't like the word equality so much because there are some things that won't be equal for a long time. I'm interested in thinking about questions like justice, because what does it mean to have justice in a household where the man may continue to make more money than the woman? When we think about day-to-day life in most homes in our society, people believe that the person who makes the most money has the right to set the order of the day—that they have the right to determine how life is structured. And I think that part of what feminism never did in a deep enough way was give people strategies in everyday life for justice, for gender justice.

I was involved for quite some time with a younger person, a younger man who didn't make as much money as I did, [and] we worked hard to come up with ways to maintain a sense of justice, because the idea that we could suddenly have equality—I mean, how could I have equality with someone who's 16 years younger than me, who was at the time just graduating from college? So justice to me is a much more

profound way to try to think about how you create equity, a
sense of sharing resources in something that is structured in
a way that is not equal. I think a lot of this fear people had
about feminism had to do with the fact that the vision of
equality as it was articulated by reformist feminism was really
not very practical for everyday life.

JERVIS: What are some things that we can do to revise
those reformist feminism theories and create strategies for
gender justice?

HOOKS: Not just to revise them but to create a whole new
body of work that is practically oriented, that tries to say,
"This is what visionary feminist thinking can do in daily life,"
starting with children. You know, one of the reasons I began
to write children's books is that I feel that feminism long ago
sort of turned its back on children. When the contemporary
feminist movement first began, for example, there was a major
critique of children's books and the kinds of images children
were receiving very early on. And if you think about *Harry
Potter* books as emblematic of where we are, even though
those books are written by a woman they tend to be very tra-
ditionally sexist, very imperialist and racist in the sense that
once again we have our little European white-boy hero. And
I'm not here trying to say those books are not enjoyable or
valuable, but they certainly don't offer a paradigm that breaks
with conventional thinking. And the question to me isn't so
much, *Why are the* Harry Potter *books so well-received?* but:
Why aren't other books that are alternative, that offer different kinds of visions, just as popular? Because we do know that

a very patriarchal, white male-dominated mass media really pushed the *Harry Potter* books. I forget which of the leading magazines—I can't remember whether it was *Newsweek* or *Time*—had the *Harry Potter* stuff on the cover. It was because certain kinds of white men in power like these books. People say to me, "Well, children really love them." I say, Well, guess what? Children wouldn't have known anything about what some white female in England is writing without a powerful partriarchally based mass media that really hyped these books.

And one of the constant struggles for feminist thinking and writing and our visions is that we rarely have access to that kind of powerful mainstream media. There are wonderful visionary feminist books that no one reads. They don't get hyped.

JERVIS: I love your idea about a feminist marketing firm.

HOOKS: Firms, firms. Because we need to take into consideration the specificity of the communities that we're in. I find it interesting, for example, that a movie like *Nurse Betty* has been getting really, really negative...people dismiss it. And yet what was awesome to me was that it had, really, a feminist message. I mean, that moment in the film where she is told that her value lies within herself and not within needing to find some fantasy recognition outside herself, whether it's Hollywood or the male gaze or what have you—that's a pretty powerful message. And I can't help but contrast it to a movie like *The Tao of Steve*, which I think is totally bankrupt and totally patriarchal. That guy doesn't reconstruct himself in any way, yet he gets the woman in the end. And yet which movie is being raved about as a great little movie? I thought *Nurse Betty* was incredible because of its gender, race, class stuff. There's a lot of stuff in it about mirroring and just the whole question of how we think about someone who is different from ourselves, how we think about people that we consider to be dumb, how much television dominates our lives.

I'm really excited, because I've come back from being on the road with *Feminism Is for Everybody*. Seeing these incredible audiences of diverse people coming out because they feel they can talk about the kinds of concerns that I'm raising. Because feminism has been established for a long time as a political movement, people are less initially hostile to the very idea, so that I think we have much more of a creative space to think of new ways of reaching people. I think of some of the questions people asked me the other night about childraising and feminism or relationships and feminism that I can't imagine people asking—well, not can't imagine people, people *did not ask*—20 years ago because it would have been considered so politically incorrect to stand up and say, "I'm having sex with this man and I don't really feel good about it. I feel like there is some element of rape even though I really love him and he really cares for me." When someone says that to me in the audience of almost a thousand people, I say to her, "Well, you know, there's a lot of other ways to be sexual than someone putting his penis in you." And the whole audience clapped, and so right there that person has this affirmation for [the notion that] there's a way to do sex, liberatory sexuality, beyond our traditional sexist-defined fixation on the penis.

I think that there is a kind of feminism that years ago would have shamed that woman for still wanting to be with a man. For still wanting to engage the penis. I think we still need to engage the penis a whole lot more [laughs], because I think we still have not changed our thinking about the penis, and until we do, until we can celebrate the penis both in its erect and its non-erect state, I don't think we'll ever have a liberatory sexuality for straight or gay people.

JERVIS: And how would we go about doing that without still making the penis the focus of what we celebrate about sexuality?

HOOKS: I think, one, that we need to see more images of the penis. A lot of times I go about my daily life thinking about sex and [being] so aware of how thinking about the breast as a sexual location of the body is so normalized, but there is nothing equivalent to that about the penis. In fact, in the last few years we have had more films, whether we're talking about *Boogie Nights* or the French film where the guy pulls out his penis and pees on the other guy, I'm forgetting the name of it… I remember sitting in the theater—it's the first scene and being really taken aback because there was a penis and the camera was really focusing on it. It was in a film that really dealt with questions of class and hierarchy and I think all of that kind of normalization of the penis in everyday life takes away that sense of threat. I think [changing the language that we use to talk about the penis has] to be part of our renewed feminist transformative visions of sexuality.

I think sexuality is the location where feminism stopped, in a sense. The Barnard conference [*"Towards a Politics of Sexuality," a 1982 conference that was the site of tremendous feminist disagreement about what feminist sexuality could be—Eds.*] and the struggle around lesbian SM—the recognition that there was such a thing as lesbian SM—in a sense so shattered all of those little notions that somehow women never want to dominate or that rough sex is something that men want to do. It was almost as if feminism couldn't go on from there, because people could not deal adequately with the whole question of power and desire. So definitely I feel that sexuality and love should be the two central issues of a revised feminism because I think that so much feminist backlash and retrograde shit is taking place in the arena of intimate relationships, particularly in heterosexual relationships. I am amazed that I can have these brilliant women students who I think of as sometimes even intellectually way beyond a bell hooks because the lives that they have led have not been like mine. Where I had to move from patriarchal sexism and repression into freedom, many of them have been in certain states of freedom— and then all of a sudden they'll get involved with some guy and it's like they never knew anything about feminism, they never knew anything about women getting married early and having babies and being stuck with the childcare. And I'm seeing a lot of that and I'm thinking, What is this? Haven't we already seen this script and seen how it ends? And yet I see masses of my female students, some of the best and the brightest, obsessing continually about marriage and "Am I going to get a man?" And the recent news of Gloria Steinem's marriage is very, very exciting in a way, the idea that a woman over 60 can be free to act relationally in ways that we don't imagine, but on the other hand I worry that it will be read culturally as a sign that, even for feminists, at the end of the day marriage is what *really* matters.

JERVIS: Well, I'm a little more optimistic than you are, in that I hope that Steinem's marriage will be read as an opening up of marriage, a flexibility—that you don't have to go out and snag that man before you turn 25.

HOOKS: I think that's the positive feminist interpretation, but I think we have a concrete way that this act has been represented by patriarchal mass media, and I kept thinking, What if Gloria Steinem could have taken the news of her marriage to a feminist marketing firm and said, "I want to have control over how this is represented. Before mainstream, patriarchal, white-supremacist capitalist mass media gets ahold of this, I want to project it in certain kinds of ways." Then I think we could say it would have that more radical impact. I think what we see is mass media representing it as, Oh, here's this feminist who always mocked marriage, but at the end of the day, look who's getting married. You have to think about how the news is reaching ordinary people. I hear a lot of feedback from people out in the world and a lot of it is more this sense that ok, this is another sign that feminism is over. I still think it's important for people to have a sharp, ongoing critique of marriage in patriarchal society—because once you marry within a society that remains patriarchal, no matter how alternative you want to be within your unit, there is still a culture outside you that will impose many, many values on you whether you want them to or not.

JERVIS: I got married two years ago, and people get this idea in their heads about what that means. To constantly be correcting those preconceived notions is a project.

HOOKS: When you live with a man in patriarchal society it's really easy to be rewarded within certain kinds of heterosexist norms. I certainly see the contrast living as a woman by myself and interacting with a very powerful world most of the time. When people ask me, "Do you want to marry?" I say, "Well, I feel that I don't want to live with a man again in the same house." I'd like him to have the apartment next to mine, because I think that the force of patriarchal society is so strong—just in daily life and who gets up to do what. When I was with a younger man, many, many people got in my face and discussed whether I was dominating him or pussy-whipping him and I kept thinking, Gosh, if every older man in patriarchy had to deal with people questioning him when he dated a younger woman, we might see some intervention around that kind of patriarchal exploitation of younger women. But I think that people felt free to do that with me because I was a woman. In fact, people *don't* feel free to go up to men and question them about their choices.

JERVIS: No, because it's not "deviant" for the man to be the one with the power, whether that comes from age or class or something else.

HOOKS: And—as I was saying earlier—because he was and is a very quiet man, many people assumed I was silencing him. And it was hard for us to constantly try to intervene on the very sexist ways people had of interpreting our relationship. And I think it's even harder when you're married to someone to try to keep a spirit of mutuality alive when other people are always seeing you outside that, through a conventional lens.

I have friends who've gotten married and suddenly people refer to them constantly through their husbands, as if they no longer existed as selves. That is so a big issue and I think the younger a woman is, the more it's an issue. Because the fact is, an exciting old hag like bell hooks is really set in her ways, so that [now] I don't feel like I would be dominated by those mores, as I might have been in my 20s—and was. Even though I had this incredible alternative relationship, it was really still impinged upon by patriarchal norms.

I think even for Gloria Steinem, many more people will be open to her because they see her by this very gesture as entering a conventional mainstream, because of the conventional sense of marriage. That is a critique we should bring to bear on feminism. Feminism hasn't changed our image of marriage. Where is our feminist *Bride's* magazine? Let's not act like rituals like weddings and bondings aren't important, but let's valorize how we do them differently—and we haven't done that.

JERVIS: There has been some feminist attention to single-hood lately, things like Marcelle Clements's book *The Improvised Woman*, which is about the pleasures of constructing your own single identity. It's time to bring that kind of attitude to relationships.

HOOKS: I'm very much interested in how we project a different kind of relationship to the world. We find ourselves best and are fully actualized in a circle of love, and that's a kind of feminist model that challenges the idea of a couple being at the center. I would very much like to be in a primary partnership that lasts for the rest of my life, but have that partnership within a community of love, a circle of love, where the partnership is one point on the circle but not everything in the circle. I think we need to hear more about how people concretely do that in daily life.

I travel a lot. My ex worked 40 hours a week all the time; it was very, very hard for him to come with me and have the level of leisure [I had], because while I worked very hard I also had much more playtime than him. Shouldn't we have at least four or five feminist magazines right now that deal with just those sorts of politics: How do we have feminist mutuality in everyday life? How do you create a balance in a relationship where one person is gone a lot? I have a male friend whose wife works out of the city half-time, and he and I were seeing each other for dinner once a week. All three of us are feminist and all of us are alternative, but she felt like, Wait a minute, there's this intense intimacy building here, I'm uncomfortable with it. We haven't discussed those things. While we talk about adultery or those kinds of issues, we don't talk about the whole question of time and intimacy and how it affects us.

Obviously, love is my big, big issue. I said years ago in *Yearning* that I'm interested in issues that bring people together. As much as we talk about the issues and things that divide people, I do feel that the yearning for love, the longing for love, cuts across class, race, sexual preferences, even cultural experiences and nationality. I've been looking at issues that potentially serve to bring people together to think differently about domination, as opposed to always looking at what divides us and separates us. I think it's often harder to articulate, What are our yearnings that are common, how do those yearnings affect us, and how can we know each other beyond our differences by starting with what we share? And what many of us share is our longing for love and being loved. And we also, through that, can understand other ways of thinking about domination, and that's really crucial.

JERVIS: Love is so often seen as a women's issue, like men don't long for love.

HOOKS: The issue is not that men don't long for love, because in fact I find many men talking just as much as women about the desire to be loved. What I find in patriarchal culture is that it's very difficult for men to talk about their longing to love or to talk about the fact that many of them feel like they don't have a clue what it means to be loving. If we go back to this model of "It's ok for men to cheat," just saying as I did to people in *All About Love*—what other people before me have said—that you can't love people and lie to them, [that] cuts right through this whole notion that somehow you can be really loving somebody while you cheat. Which is not to say that you couldn't make a mutual decision to have non-monogamy.

One of the things that I know from being in mutual bonds that have been nonmonogamous is that you don't have anymore the thrill or the danger that comes from betrayal. When you have a mutual relationship with someone that is rooted in peace and love and justice, a lot of the old charges, the stimulants and how they can up the tension level but be a downer in the long run [are taken away]—if you think about cheating as a kind of crack. I think that people are often afraid to have open, honest communication because in the act of being open and honest, you lose a lot of those tensions that come through the eroticizing of negative sadomasochism and dominance.

JERVIS: Eroticizing communication and mutuality hasn't really been done, certainly not within pop culture.

HOOKS: Well, we need to speak that eroticism, because I think many of us feel that we are living in it. Sex is better within feminism. I tell that and I see it in my life all the time—that women and men who have a sense of justice, who claim their sexual agency, have what I can see is the most fun, exciting sex that there is. Because what could be more exciting than that touch and that bonding with another human being that allows you to know a certain kind of divine glory?

HOW DO YOU PRACTICE INTERSECTIONALISM? AN INTERVIEW WITH BELL HOOKS

INTERVIEW BY DON JENNINGS,
NOM DE PLUME RANDY LOWENS
BLACK ROSE ANARCHIST FEDERATION
MAY 5, 2011

This interview originally appeared in *Northeastern Anarchist* #15 in 2011—In June of 2009 bell hooks agreed to be interviewed. We met at a local coffee shop and, over bagels and espresso drinks, discussed her books, politics and thoughts on recent events such as the economic downturn. I found her as forthright in person as on the page and with a subtle wit not always apparent (to me) in her writing. For example, after the interview we were approached by a local lawyer who was curious what publication she was being interviewed for. She cut her eyes at me and said, "Tell the man who the interview is for." Upon learning I was anarchist, the lawyer mouthed familiar clichés about disorganization. hooks, a hint of a grin playing at the corners of her mouth, responded, "Yes, yes, it's all about license for the individual!"

RANDY LOWENS: We're interviewing bell hooks, author of *Feminist Theory: From Margin to Center*, *Outlaw Culture: Resisting Representations* and numerous other titles. You're known to be a prolific author: Do you have a personal favorite? Is there any one title that someone unfamiliar with your work should read first?

BELL HOOKS: My work is so eclectic; it spans such a broad spectrum. I guess if you look at my children's books, I like

Be Boy Buzz the best. If you look at the love books, I like *All About Love* the best. If you look at the theory books, *Where We Stand: Class Matters* is one of my favorites. It's a good thing not to have to choose one. I think part of Western metaphysical dualism is, we're always being asked to choose one over the other. I'm lucky. I think it's good that I have a body of work that addresses different things in different ways.

LOWENS: You don't capitalize your name? Why is that?

HOOKS: When the feminist movement was at its zenith in the late '60s and early '70s, there was a lot of moving away from the idea of the person. It was: let's talk about the ideas behind the work, and the people matter less. It was kind of a gimmicky thing, but lots of feminist women were doing it. Many of us took the names of our female ancestors—bell hooks is my maternal great-grandmother—to honor them and debunk the notion that we were these unique, exceptional women. We wanted to say, actually, we were the products of the women who'd gone before us.

LOWENS: The books of yours I'm most familiar with—the two I cited—are a work of political theory and, the other, a work of cultural criticism. Do you see those as distinctly different? Is there any clear line between the cultural and the political?

HOOKS: I would say one difference with the political writings, whether about feminism or class, is that the intent is to change how people think of a certain political reality; whereas with cultural criticism, the goal is to illuminate something that is already there. For example, the contemporary movie *Crash* I thought was a very weak statement about race and class. That was already there in the film. What I did in having a conversation about it was illuminate why it was a weak analysis of race and class. "It's people; we're all racist." That's just another bullshit way of people not wanting to name the power and institutionalized strength of white supremacy. We all may have prejudices, but we're not all part of a system that reinforces, reinvents and reaffirms itself every day of our lives, systemically.

LOWENS: You mentioned your children's books. I think last time we spoke, you were preparing to publish a book, *Happy to Be Nappy*?

HOOKS: *Happy to Be Nappy* was my first children's book. I think when we saw each other I was in the production of *Grump Groan Growl* which was about anger.

LOWENS: I read that one to my daughter, by the way.

HOOKS: Oh yeah?

LOWENS: Do you have anything to say about the distinction? Are these books in any way political? We have a political audience.

HOOKS: They absolutely are. Both books were written to counter racism, patriarchy or both. Especially *Be Boy Buzz* was written to say, "We don't really live in a culture that loves boys or loves children, and we don't encourage boys to be whole." I wanted to write a nonpatriarchal book that would proclaim the love of boys.

LOWENS: [*pause*] Some of my questions are written kind of wordy. [*laughter*]

HOOKS: You shouldn't worry about that.

LOWENS: You're known, especially within our circles, for popularizing intersectional theory as opposed to reductionisms. Can you say a little bit about how intersectional theory plays out in practice? That is to say, your typical class reductionist at least has a priority; a Black Nationalist has something to prioritize. How do you practice intersectionalism?

HOOKS: Intersectionality allow us to focus on what is most important at a given point in time. I used to say to people, if you're in a domestic situation where the man is violent, patriarchy and male domination—even though you understand it intersectionally—you focus, you highlight that dimension of it, if that's what is needed to change the situation. I think that, again, if we move away from either/or thinking, and if we think, okay, every day of my life that I walk out of my house I am a combination of race, gender, class, sexual preference and religion or what have you, what gets foregrounded? I think it's crazy for us to think that people don't understand what's being foregrounded in their lives at a given point in time. Like right now, for many Americans, class is being foregrounded like never before because of the economic situation. It doesn't mean that race doesn't matter, or gender doesn't matter, but it means that right now in many people's lives, in the lives of my own family members, people are losing jobs, insurance. I was teasing my brother that he was penniless, homeless, jobless. Right now in his life, racism isn't the central highlighting force: it's the world of work and economics. It doesn't mean that he isn't influenced by racism, but when he wakes up in the morning the thing that's driving his world is really issues of class, economics and power as they articulate themselves. I guess I wish we could talk about: what does it mean to have a politics of intersectionality that also privileges what form of domination is most oppressing us at a given moment in time.

LOWENS: I'm reminded of Murray Bookchin and the analogy of society to ecology. Were you at all influenced by that?

HOOKS: No.

LOWENS: Do you have any opinions of the modern-day anarchist movement, globally or here in the U.S.A.? It's almost nonexistent here in the South.

HOOKS: Sadly, anarchy has gotten such a bad name. We don't really see much evidence of it because people associate it with reckless abandon, which we both know it's not. I think we have to talk about educating the people for critical consciousness about what anarchy is. I would also say that, in practice, many more Americans are anarchists than would ever use that term.

LOWENS: It's clear from your books that you oppose capitalism. Do you think capitalism can be reformed, or must it be over-thrown? Do you consider yourself a revolutionary in that sense?

HOOKS: I see myself, in terms of the question of capitalism, as I would support democratic socialism over a capitalist system, because any approach . . . or participatory economics, which is another great model that people like Michael Albert are putting out there . . . any system that encourages us to think about interdependency, and to be able to use the world's resources in a wiser way, for the good of the whole, would be better for the world than capitalism. Capitalism is fucking up the planet, we know that. But let's say, imperialism and capitalism together . . . I mean let's face it, war in its essence is another form of capitalism. Wars make people rich—and they make a lot of people poor, and they take a lot of people's lives away from them. We know that so much of the war that is happening is the attempt of one group to snatch the resources of another group.

LOWENS: Competitive economics taken to its logical extreme.

HOOKS: Exactly.

LOWENS: I was taken to task by a feminist anarchist for taking the liberty of referring to you by your first name. The criticism was: had you been a male I wouldn't have been so quick to have done that.

HOOKS: I think this is the kind of trivial personal stuff people focus on that has very little meaning. I don't think it matters. To me, I think if someone read my work, they'd know I don't have issues around how I'm identified. Even when people capitalize my name, I don't freak out, even though that would not be my choice. I'm not attached to it, and in that sense I think we have to choose: What are the issues that really matter? We have to trust that. You have to trust that if you are calling my name in a way that is offensive to me, I'm going to share it with you. But you also have to know what your feelings are behind calling me "bell." I think we are obsessed in the U.S. with the personal, in ways that blind us to more important issues of life. I just think if we could take all the obsession with the personal [*inaudible*], and personal judgment and have people be concerned about the environment, what a different world we would live in. Or race . . . ending racism. It's like, I was talking about Cornel West once, and somebody was saying to me, "Cornel is not a preacher; he's not ordained"—and another preacher friend of mine said, "I don't know about the importance of his being ordained. I saw him give a sermon. Lots of people joined the church and that would seem to be what being a preacher is all about." We have to look at the substance of something rather than the shadow. Is it more important that you, as a white male, read my work and learn from it, or what you call me? I think it's more important that you read my work, reflect on it, and allow it to transform your life and your thinking in some way. Now I do get a little pissed at people who write me and want me to do things, and spell my name wrong.

LOWENS: I have read, from someone else, that your work is influenced by postmodernism. Is that true? Do you have an opinion about the end of history, in particular?

HOOKS: No. If anything I think postmodernism has the least impact on my work. My work is mostly influenced by the concrete circumstances of our daily lives. To the extent that we live in a postmodern world and it shapes the concrete circumstances of our daily lives, I would say postmodernism affects my work or influences my work. But in general, I don't spend a lot of time thinking about postmodernism.

LOWENS: The final question that I wrote down, I think we've already touched on to a certain degree. Some political groups say they are against classism, and that often sounds to me like they're saying they avoid prejudice on the basis of class, but don't oppose structural capitalism. I think you've already talked about the personal versus the systemic aspects of . . .

HOOKS: One of the things my work *Where We Stand: Class Matters* tried to do was say, "We're a country that would rather talk about race than class." I think what's so amazing about this historical moment is that it is bringing class to the fore and we have to think about the nature of work and hierarchy. When I think about the auto industry and how it was one of the industries that brought all of these Black men from the South to Michigan and other places to make more money than they could ever make in the cotton fields or the agricultural world of the South . . . what's happening now is all of that is closing down, and we know that it's going to reopen in Southern places, focusing on Mexican and other migrant workers to come and work cheaply and get none of the benefits. All of this stuff is amazing in terms of forcing people in this society to think more openly about class and about the intersectionalities.

The whole thing with Joe the Plumber—and then to find out that so much about Joe the Plumber was just fake—was the use of class (of white supremacy and class) to awaken old prejudices, to allow for a denial of the true impact of intersectionalities and class. The white worker who has been displaced at General Motors has more in common with the displaced Black worker than those larger white CEOs, and those Wall Street people who are determining their fate . . . whose thievery and greed is determining their fate.

It's interesting to look at all the aspects where everyday Americans, many of whom are not college educated, are thinking deeply now about our economic structure. See the way credit cards have exploited the working class and the working poor? I think it's going to be an interesting next ten years for the United States. For people like me, what is important and vital is to keep that education for critical consciousness around intersectionalities, so that people are able to not focus on one thing and blame one group, but be able to look holistically at the way intersectionality informs all of us: whiteness, gender, sexual preferences, etc. Only then can we have a realistic handle on the political and cultural world we live within.

LOWENS: That's all of my questions. Do you have anything to say to our audience, off the cuff?

HOOKS: Dare to look at the intersectionalities. Dare to be holistic. Part of the heart of anarchy is, dare to go against the grain of the conventional ways of thinking about our realities. Anarchists have always gone against the grain, and that's been a place of hope.

HILLBILLY SOLID
RADIO INTERVIEW

INTERVIEW BY SILAS HOUSE
HILLBILLY SOLID
NOVEMBER 2012

SILAS HOUSE: You're listening to *Hillbilly Solid* with your host, me, Silas House, here on listener-supported radio at WUKY. We are very honored to be talking to bell hooks today. I'm very lucky to count bell as a friend and a neighbor in the little town of Berea, Kentucky, where we are both on the faculty of Berea College.

bell was born Gloria Jean Watkins in Hopkinsville, Kentucky, but is known by her pen name, bell hooks, which is intentionally uncapitalized and is in tribute to her maternal grandmother, Bell Blair Hooks.

bell is the author of more than thirty books, including the very recently published *Appalachian Elegy*, a book of poetry from the University Press of Kentucky. bell is a feminist, a social activist, and one of our greatest public intellectuals. bell's writing focuses on race, capitalism, sexuality, gender, class, and oppression, among other issues. Her work has been hugely influential and visionary, and her book *Ain't I a Woman: Black Women and Feminism* is widely seen as one of the most important books of the last fifty years.

Thanks so much for being on with us today, bell.

BELL HOOKS: I'm happy to be talking. You know us Kentuckians love an opportunity to talk.

HOUSE: [*laughs*] Oh anytime, anytime. We want to focus on your new book, but before that, I had just a few general questions for you. You and I can talk for two or three hours easy; I wish we had longer. But one thing I wanted to ask you about is one of my favorite quotes is by Erica Jong, and she says, "To change one's name is the first act of the poet and the revolutionary." Now you changed your name—and I also go by a different name than I went by growing up— and I think it's very fair to say that you are both a poet and a revolutionary. So I'm wondering how do you respond to that quote?

HOOKS: Well, I respond to that quote by, you know, recognizing that names have power, and the name I was born with really does—Gloria Jean, given to me—really reflects how much my parents wanted me to be a very feminine, Southern belle type girl, and I think that in order to find my voice and use it, I had to use the name of my great-grandmother on a maternal side—bell hooks—in order to bring a self into being that my parents and my home were not nurturing.

HOUSE: Can you tell us about why you don't capitalize it?

HOOKS: Well, you know, people forget that early on in the late '60s and early '70s, especially among people engaged with feminism, there was all of this talk about getting rid of the ego. You know, we weren't just engaged with feminism, we were engaged in all these Eastern religions, sexual liberation, and the whole idea of divorcing oneself from the ego. Paying attention to who is speaking was, you know, politically incorrect; the point was to listen to what people were saying. So lots of people in those days engaged with feminism used pseudonyms or different names. In my case, you know, I have an essay about this . . . I say, when the name bell hooks is called, the spirit of my great-grandmother rises because it also had to do with how many of us were not able to name the female lineage that we came from.

HOUSE: Sort of similar to that, this show is called *Hillbilly Solid*, of course, and we've received some criticism for using the H word. I want to claim that word for myself and for my people; I want the power of that word to be in our hands—sort of just the same thing you're talking about with names—and I have heard you use the word "hillbilly" in a positive way too. So, can you talk a little bit about why you choose to do that?

HOOKS: Well, you know, just the other night I did a big reading and someone came up afterwards—an older white man—and told me, you know, how many folks in his family had been hurt by being called "hillbilly." And, you know, it's really a difficult thing because it depends on your standpoint. You know? Because where I came from, one was hillbilly and proud. So much of my work is about trying to remind people of the history of African Americans in the hills of Kentucky, both eastern and western Kentucky, and so the idea that we would be seen as hillbillies, that would be like, okay, we've arrived, people are recognizing our presence. But like you, Silas, I want to reclaim it at the same time that I am troubled when someone tells me that it is very wounding to them. I think it is like all the words—like "nigger" or "dyke"—or all the words that we hope to shed the poisonous, toxic energy of those words and see if they can be transformed. I think there is a lot of hope for "hillbilly." And I think the reason we have to hold on to it is we've gotta have the counter-hegemonic hillbilly to counter the very foolish vision of hillbillies that continues to be alive and well in our society. I mean, I just wrote a long critique of the film *Beasts of the Southern Wild*, and then I read an incredibly exciting critique by Dudley Cox, who is head of the Appalachian Theatre, and he likened it to all the images of hillbillies—all the films that have been made that show the little wild kid—and that was really deep for me, to see that there was this trajectory. I feel like we both have to deconstruct "hillbilly" and claim "hillbilly" at the same time.

HOUSE: Exactly. Yeah, the hillbilly characters and the little Black children are always nasty, you know; it never fails in films it seems like. I definitely noticed that in *Beasts of the Southern Wild*. There was a recent movie set in Appalachia—I think it was called *Lawless*—it was just like the hillbilly characters are always dirty, living in trash.

Another thing I wanted to ask you about before we get more into the book is . . . lots of writers nowadays feel that using a word like "love" is passé, that it's precious, and that they are just much too sophisticated and jaded for using that word. But you have actively used the word "love" in your writing and lectures, and I appreciate that so much about your work—the way that you use that word. I'm wondering how consciously you have chosen to do that.

HOOKS: Well, really, it's a conscious political choice because when I looked around in the world and I saw where transformation was taking place, whether it was eco-feminism, environmentalism, I saw that the deepest experiences of change and transformation came where there was love. I mean, I've been telling everyone that they have to see *A Fierce Green Fire*, which is a documentary of the environmental movement. When you see those young white people in their little boats, putting their bodies between the whales and the harpoons, there is such love there. I mean, it moves you. I don't know that there's been an experience—visual experience—where I have felt as connected to a white social activist, and because, you know, I don't swim, I don't whitewater raft, but I was so moved by this . . . this is the courage to love that Dr. King talks about, the strength to love, and this is not some "sentimental Hallmark card" kind of love. This is the transformative love that we are going to have to evoke in this world to heal our planet and to heal our souls.

HOUSE: This to me is among the many important things you do—that idea and the way you talk about love is so important and we need to hear so much more of that in our world today. I hope that people out there have been able to hear you at readings and lectures because you just leave a changed person because—I mean the audience member leaves a changed person—because they hear you talking about love that way, so I do appreciate that so much.

HOOKS: And, you know, it's interesting because more recently I'm trying to write about a spiritual memoir, writing about my own movement towards a more godly life, and it's been really amusing, Silas, 'cause I found people really don't want to talk about that.

HOUSE: We are speaking with bell hooks, author of *Appalachian Elegy*, here on *Hillbilly Solid* on WUKY, and let's talk more about the new book, bell, *Appalachian Elegy*. What would you like for us to know about this book that does so much of what you were just talking about?

HOOKS: Well, I want people to really hear an African American voice claiming Kentucky and claiming belonging. My critical book that is almost like a companion to those poetry books is called *Belonging: A Culture of Place*. I've been saying to people that I was like so many people growing up; I couldn't wait to leave Kentucky. Partially for me as a Black person, I just felt it was so racist here. But then I said, eventually I saw that racism was everywhere in our culture, and so I didn't have to run away from Kentucky, I could run towards Kentucky. 'Cause Kentucky offered me so many things. You know, I came back here to live after being away almost thirty years, but coming all the time to see my parents, and partially I came back here to live 'cause my parents were aging, and in the last few years, they are both deceased, but I realized that the kind of childhood I had in Kentucky, in the hills of Kentucky, were the values that have made me, that when I think about what made bell hooks, I think the first foundation is the values that people would call Appalachia, you know. I say in my little essay in the beginning, early on in my life I learned from Kentucky backwoods elders, the folks whom we might now label 'Appalachian,' a set of values rooted in the belief that above all else, one must be self-determining. It is the foundation that is the root of my radical critical consciousness. Folks from the backwoods were certain about two things: that every human soul needed to be free, and that the responsibility of being free required one to be a person of integrity, a person who lived in such a way that there would always be congruency between what one thinks, says, and does.

I was talking the other night at the Wild Fig—the wonderful bookstore that is being run by Crystal Wilkinson and Ron, her partner, Limestone—I was talking about the fact that when my work was reviewed in the early years of my career, no one mentioned that I was from Kentucky. The fact that I was an intellectual speaking to a broader audience, it was almost like it negated Kentucky. I think that I was part of that because I wanted to be this universal writer, even though, of course, Wendell Berry was a light into my past—but so was Gary Snyder, and Gary Snyder symbolized much more for me, this sort of cosmopolitan world of nature and environmentalism and Buddhism (that's where I got turned on to Buddhism, with the [*inaudible*])—and so, you know, coming back to Kentucky for me was about claiming that place of belonging. Being able to say this is where my roots are, this is the kind of person that I am because of this place. And I feel it every day; I love being in Berea, because Berea is both like and not like the place that I grew up in.

HOUSE: Exactly. Well, you've provided me with an excellent segue because my favorite poem in the book is number 6, and I think everything you were just talking about is in that poem.

I think you have a copy handy. I'm wondering if you wouldn't mind reading number 6 for us.

HOOKS: Okay.

> Listen little sister
> angels make their hope here
> in these hills
> follow me
> I will guide you
> careful now
> no trespass
> I will guide you
> word for word
> mouth for mouth
> all the holy ones
> embracing us
> all our kin
> making home here
> renegade marooned
> lawless fugitives
> grace these mountains
> we have earth to bind us
> the covenant
> between us
> can never be broken
> vows to live and let live

So you hear in that poem that insistence on being self-determining, both responsible and self-determining, that I think is so much a part of, for me, my Kentucky legacy and what I hope to leave with my students and with the people that I encounter in everyday life here.

HOUSE: Do you think it's true that writers carry around a great sadness? And do we have that sadness because we're writers, or are we writers because we have that sadness?

HOOKS: It's so interesting that you ask that, Silas, 'cause my morning meditation has to do with grief because I often feel such a tremendous sense of grief about what's happening in our world, what's happening to people around me, the disconnects, and my dysfunctional family and others. But I don't know that I think it's so much writers but people who are choosing to be aware. It's hard to wake up, in the Buddhist sense. I mean, to open your eyes and see what's happening in our world without feeling that grief. And the point that Thich Nhat Hanh always says—the Vietnamese Buddhist monk—is I gotta take that grief and use it as compost, you know, for my garden. That's the challenge for me. I feel like that grief has been with me since I was a child facing the brutal racism of Kentucky, the extreme patriarchal sexism of my parents and our religion, and, you know, just trying to find that place *of* through the pain and the sadness to a place where one can say as Jackie Wilson in his song, "Your Love Has Lifted Me Higher." That's the thing, when I go out to my land and I look out at the hills and I think about that scripture that says, "I will lift up mine eyes unto the hills, from whence cometh my help." So there again we have that evocation of nature and the environment, and that which helps us, restores us, which gives us a way to keep a hold on life. For me, it's keeping that grief balanced, but I don't know an aware person who doesn't have that grief.

HOUSE: I'm thinking another thing that I always notice you doing is that, it seems to me that you feed on every kind of art. I love that about you so much. You're such a great reader and you also love films and music, and I know that you love Bonnie "Prince" Billy, but what else are you listening to these days?

HOOKS: Well, let me say that I worship at the throne of Bonnie "Prince" Billy. You know I have this institute—the bell hooks center—for critical thinking, contemplation, and dreaming, and it's all about trying to educate people and call forth creativity away from the academy. And I think, oh, my next person—I had Gloria Steinem, but the next person I want is Bonnie "Prince" Billy. But lately I've just been super listening to Leonard Cohen, both old and new. I think because I turned sixty in September—you were there as a witness to the so-called non-party party—but I think that I have just become enchanted by listening to people like Leonard Cohen, Ramsey Lewis, who are over the age of seventy but are still creating such an amazing body of work and changing and showing us that it's never too late for reconciliation; it's never too late for us to have a burst of creativity. That's awesome to me 'cause I know I want to be creating into my grave. But I said to the audience the other night that I also . . . I think a lot about what if there's no more books in bell hooks? I mean, I don't really want to continue to write about sex, race, gender, class, because I feel like I've already set forth paradigms in all these books I've written. So I'm at a threshold of change and new direction, and, you know, I say, what if I can't write anything, can I be content with being? I mean, in September, which was my birthday month, I spent a lot of time meditating on the notion from Philippians of being content no matter your circumstance because I think that's where our power lies. And I'm looking . . . This is a new stage of life for me, Silas, so I'm just trying to . . . I just finished a bunch of poems that are very short that were inspired by the big show on the female buddha that was at the Buddhist museum in New York City. But I want to write little, short books about all kind of silly things.

HOUSE: I can't wait for your spiritual memoir.

HOOKS: You know, two books that I've read recently that just touched my spirit was, one was the older book by Natalie Goldberg, *Long Quiet Highway*, which is a kind of spiritual and creative memoir 'cause it's about her struggle to balance those two things—being a writer, being devoted to a spiritual practice. And Terry Tempest Williams's new book *When Women Were Birds*, it's just so awesome. I mean, I have to tell you, you know, reading is the absolute core pleasure of my life.

HOUSE: Right.

HOOKS: I also think that because I'm in my head so much and reading so much that's why nature matters to me. You know, when Jesus says, "I'll call you into the wilderness and there speak to you heart to heart," it's like I have to be in that world of nature, silence, away from my brain . . . thinking about theory or other things in order to restore I think the metaphor of the desert and going into the desert, and I think we need to hear more from women about our spiritual lives and about where we travel, where we journey to restore ourselves.

HOUSE: Well, thank you so much for sharing all of that with us and for sharing time with us. I know that there are many listeners out there who would love to be able to thank you for all of your good work, so I will just say it on their behalf. You do so much good work, so much that we know about and lots that nobody knows about, and we sure appreciate you. We're going to close the show with a Bonnie "Prince" Billy song just for you. Will that be all right?

HOOKS: All right, on to the blessings.

TOUGH LOVE WITH BELL HOOKS

INTERVIEW BY ABIGAIL BEREOLA
SHONDALAND
DECEMBER 13, 2017

For many women, writer and scholar bell hooks requires no introduction. The acclaimed feminist author has written more than thirty books and has made it her life's work to take on systems of oppression and domination. Her 2000 book, *Feminism Is for Everybody*, is a must-read primer on women's equality, while 1993's *Sisters of the Yam*, dives into the emotional health of Black women. In *Teaching to Transgress*, written in 1994, hooks studied education as a path toward freedom. The prolific intellectual icon even has a few children's books under her belt.

In the early 2000s, hooks published a series of books about human love and relationships—*All About Love: New Visions, Communion: The Female Search for Love, The Will to Change: Men, Masculinity, and Love*, and *Salvation: Black People and Love*—which she's said has been her favorite topic to write about. These books explore the very concept of love, along with ideas of masculinity and femininity. And, nearly twenty years after the first "love" book was released, the series remains popular and relevant—serving as an invaluable resource for everything from coming to terms with a breakup to simply sorting out what it means to care for another human.

On a Wednesday afternoon, I spoke to hooks on the phone about the deep work of self-love and how a lack of it has played into the patriarchal culture of workplace abuse and assault.

ABIGAIL BEREOLA: Throughout your books, you write specifically of "the desire to love and be loved as [being] worthy of serious study and attention." Love is something that is sought, romance permeates everything, and people are always talking about their partners or relationships, but even so, actual discussions of love and how to achieve it are often considered to be frivolous—why do you think this is?

BELL HOOKS: I think the true work of love is just so hard. It requires integrity, that there be a congruency between what we think, say, and do. I think romance has the total different feeling of "it's easy, it comes and goes," so I think that people would rather settle for a counterfeit of love than to actually do the work of love. Because the work of love is first and foremost about knowledge and knowing a person. It is not easy to get to know somebody. You don't get to know somebody in a minute. I'm always stunned by people who have met somebody and then a month later, they've either moved in or they're getting married, and I think, do you know this person?

BEREOLA: How long do you think it takes to cultivate love?

HOOKS: I think it's more how much work are you willing to put into the acts of knowing and caring. It's not really about how much time, but what are you willing to do. I think, because people are so busy and so caught up in things, it's really hard for people to think about, "OK, I just met this person that I'm really attracted to, but it may take me a year to get a sense of who that person really is."

BEREOLA: In *Communion*, you discuss female competition due to notions of scarcity—of men, of jobs, of attention, of love—and how this is a barrier to cultivating sisterhood. What do you think it takes to move away from this model? How do we begin to see that what is for us will be for us and accept that gracefully?

HOOKS: I think that's the whole project of self-love. [Your f]irst love is self-love. Self-love begins with taking that fearless inventory where you're able to go into the attic or the closet of yourself and see what's there. What do you appreciate about yourself? How do you interact with other people?

Most of us [make this] journey arduously because we are a culture of low self-esteem. Women, especially, often get caught in the trap of low self-esteem. And so, in that sense, it's really hard to trust that life is right, that you can find love, or that your life can be meaningful without love if you are talking about romantic partnership.

I don't have a partner. I've been celibate for seventeen years. And I would love to have a partner, but I don't think that my life is less meaningful. I always tell people my life is a pie and there's a slice of the pie that's missing, but there's so much pie left over—do I really want to spend my time looking at that empty piece and judging myself by that? That's a key thing in female competition, too, that we're always judging. Years ago, we used to have this practice within feminist circles of "Can you go a whole day as a woman without making some critical judgments of yourself?" Without even thinking, there's this constant flow of negative judgment and that is just so counter to love. And so, then we of course assume that every other female is doing it to us.

When I was reading *The Will to Change: Men, Masculinity, and Love* in preparation for talking with you—I hadn't read it in a couple years—I was like, "bell hooks, this is a really good book and I think that you should just close this book and take some time in silence to be thankful to the divine for your really smart mind and for the gift of these thoughts." I don't think I would have been able to do that twenty years ago. I would have had some notion that, "Oh, you're so full of yourself," rather than "I can have an honest assessment of my value." Women will love each other more and our daughters and people more if we can have that honest assessment.

BEREOLA: In *All About Love*, you write about how common it is to try to find someone who can love the flaws that you can't. But in *The Will to Change*, you also discuss how, with regard to masculinity and love, men often feed into the avoidance of intimacy through abusive tactics. So I'm wondering, since the intimate partners of men can often end up being the keepers of their vulnerability, but also the keepers of their rage, as you say, do you feel that it is more acceptable for men to have and show their flaws in intimate relationships than it is for women?

HOOKS: I think, especially, it is okay for a man to show his flaws to the woman he's involved with. I don't think men are particularly open to showing their flaws in relationships that are not intimate, because they want to be safe. Whereas women are made to feel that we aren't safe and that, in fact, we might feel that we'll be safer if we acknowledge flaws, if we have an assumption of vulnerability. "I'm not good at—." "I make mistakes," or what have you. That that will, in fact, ease our way in the world. I don't think men think that that will ease their way in the world.

BEREOLA: It's easy to think of chemistry as being a foundation of love, but in *All About Love*, you caution us away from that line of thought. You tell us that love is an action, and a choice. But what about choosing to love someone who doesn't choose to love you? Can that also be a form of perfect love or is perfect love always mutual?

HOOKS: I can love somebody who doesn't love me, but I can't have a relationship of love with somebody who doesn't love me. It's very hard to hold to loving someone who is not going to love you. I remember when I was in this relationship with a younger man and he had made a decision that he didn't want to love me and I kept wanting him to love me. I would say to my therapist, "Well, I'm going to go over to his place," and she said, "Well, you know, I think it's fine if you're going over to his place for friendship, but if you're going over there looking for love, you're not going to find it because that's not something he is able to give and he doesn't want to work at giving it to you." Those were really harsh truths to hear, but they were true. I'm still friends with this person today, even though we broke up years ago, because I stopped expecting him to give me something that he didn't want to give me or that he might have just been completely incapable of giving.

BEREOLA: In *All About Love*, you discuss perfect love as a state of refining as opposed to something that is inherently there. What do you think that process of refining can look like over time?

HOOKS: I think it is so much about acceptance of self and other. I'm always amazed by how much we don't accept. I was talking in our group about longtime married people, like people who are married thirty years, and you still will find in many of those—especially heteronormative relationships—this thread of dissatisfaction with the other person or annoyance with the other person. I know my parents had it, and they were married for way more than thirty years. But it's like there was never that moment of acceptance of that person as being who they are. Because also accepting someone as they are may mean also that you have to accept that they can't be what you want them to be and I think that's really hard for us. We want to make people be what we want them to be.

As I look at young women, looking for love in heteronormative relationships, the first question that comes up with them and guys is not qualities of being, like, "Are you kind?" It's, "First of all, are you cute?" And then it's, "What does he do?" And I'm guilty of this, too, with all my feminism. A lot of people don't agree with me, but I actually believe that men are just as unhappy in relationships as women within patriarchy. Because studies show that most men across race, across class, across economics, choose a female partner based on liking their looks. You hear guys talk about, "Oh yeah, the moment I saw her I knew. That was the woman I was going to marry." But they're really talking about some deep attraction they had to this person's physicality. Not to qualities of being. Often in heteronormative spaces, if the man is not exhibiting patriarchal masculinity, people will say, "Oh bell, he's gay." Which I think is probably one of the fiercest barriers to heterosexual men challenging patriarchy, the fear that they will be perceived as gay. The homophobia that lies underneath that. And we see that the self-actualized man or self-loving man isn't afraid of being perceived as gay because he knows who he is. If he's gay, that's fine, if he's not, that's fine. But I think in general, most men do not allow themselves that freedom to be fully self-actualized.

BEREOLA: What do you think it would take for men to become fully self-actualized?

HOOKS: A lot of this stuff begins in childhood. And I think until we really look at how patriarchy and how domination influences how we raise boys, I don't think we're going to see a lot of change. It can't begin when somebody's thirty or twenty.

When I think about grown men masturbating in front of somebody, I think these were the boys that got some weird messages when they were ten or whatever and they're acting out. It's funny, people will psychologize some man who walked into a church and killed twenty people, but they won't psychologize men who are guilty of sexual misconduct in that way and think, well, what happened to them? What created this need, this desire? It's not normalized because if it were, more people would be doing it. But we don't really want to look at the hearts of males—boys and men—because we'd have to see what patriarchal domination has done.

BEREOLA: You wrote these three books in the early 2000s. What do you think has changed in American culture with regard to love and what do you think remains the same? Have you had changes of opinion with regard to any of your thoughts on the subject?

HOOKS: The one thing I see now is that if you make the choice to love yourself and others, how much harder—in terms of finding partnership or finding even a circle of people to be with—it is. I was kind of stunned reading *The Will to Change* that so much of what was being said there was so true of right now. It feels like there hadn't been a great deal of movement on the part of the collectivity of maleness in our society and that was, needless to say, very disturbing.

I would say that I think in terms of feminist politics and feminist practice, that the world changed most for women in relation to work, but that really, in relation to the family—of any family we're talking about—not a lot really changed. I see women today working full-time jobs but still doing most of the household work, still doing most of the care of children. I know many more women living alone, especially women over forty, because they've had incredibly unkind, cruel, and abusive relationships with men, and they just don't intend to experience that again and again and again. But I don't see them living alone as a statement of power and self-actualization. It's almost like a form of self-protection. I don't really think we talk about that.

Most guys are patriarchal which means they don't even have their own self-love as the central aspect of their lives. So we're not going to get the self-love that they don't have to give. Personally, I think they need to be in therapeutic camps where they are taught how to love. I always liked that moment in that movie, *Thelma and Louise*, when one of them says when a woman is crying, she's not having a good time. And it just felt like this is just such a basic level of emotional awareness and to think that there's so many men who don't have that.

BEREOLA: I saw something interesting on Twitter the other day that basically—somebody had said that all the charming men that they had ever known had been abusers.

HOOKS: But see, I would say most of the men we know have an abuser inside them because patriarchy has trained them from childhood on, and so, the nicest man can get in a situation where that abuser can all of a sudden come to life. Like with my young ex who had always been such a mild-mannered guy but as we were in the breaking up process became so angry hostile, and I think that's how we don't want to acknowledge what patriarchy does to the inner life of males, of boys and men.

BEREOLA: Do you think it's possible to achieve a loving society, particularly in this era? What do you think that would look like?

HOOKS: I think that societies begin with our small units of community, which are family—whether bio or chosen. I am often amazed when I meet people that I see have been raised in loving families because they're so different and they live in the world differently. I don't agree that every family is dysfunctional—I think we don't want to admit that when people are loving, it's a different world. It's an amazing world. It's a world of peace. It's not that they don't have pain, but they know how to handle their pain in a way that's not self-negating. And so I think insomuch as we begin to look again at the family and challenging and changing patriarchy within family systems, irrespective of what those families are, there's hope for love.

BELL HOOKS (1952-2021) was a trailblazer. She was a prolific American author, feminist theorist, social activist, cultural critic, and professor, whose work examined the connections between race, gender, and class. Born Gloria Jean Watkins, hooks used her pen name to pay homage to her great-grandmother, Bell Blair Hooks, whom hooks was often compared to when she was growing up. She chose to lowercase it to center attention on her ideas and establish her own identity.

She wrote over thirty books, among them *Feminist Theory: From Margin to Center*; *Talking Back: Thinking Feminist, Thinking Black*; *All About Love: New Visions*; *Communion: The Female Search for Love*; *Salvation: Black People and Love*; and *Ain't I a Woman: Black Women and Feminism*.

Although hooks sparked a lot of controversy with her views, her unwavering dedication to her work forged deep grooves for the feminist and anti-racist movements, and her work continues to be as relevant today as ever.

She died on December 15, 2021, at the age of sixty-nine due to kidney failure.

MIKKI KENDALL Mikki Kendall is a writer, diversity consultant, and occasional feminist; she has appeared on the BBC, NPR, *The Daily Show*, PBS, *Good Morning America*, MSNBC, Al Jazeera, WBEZ, and Showtime, and discusses race, feminism, police violence, tech, and pop culture at institutions and universities across the country. She is the author of the New York Times-bestselling *Hood Feminism* (recipient of the Chicago Review of Books Award and named a best book of the year by BBC, *Bustle*, and *TIME*). She is also the author of *Amazons, Abolitionists, and Activists*, a graphic novel illustrated by A. D'Amico. Her essays can be found at *TIME*, the *New York Times*, *The Guardian*, the *Washington Post*, *Essence*, *Vogue*, *The Boston Globe*, NBC, and a host of other sites.

YVONNE ZYLAN is a sociologist and attorney who has taught at the University of Arizona, Hamilton College, the University of New Mexico, Thomson Rivers University Faculty of Law, and the University of British Columbia Allard School of Law. She is the author of *States of Passion: Law, Identity, and the Social Construction of Desire*, which was published by Oxford University Press in 2011. She currently works as a senior law clerk at the New Mexico Supreme Court.

HELEN TWORKOV is *Tricycle*'s founding editor and author of *Zen in America: Profiles of Five Teachers* (1989). She's also the co-author of *Turning Confusion into Clarity: A Guide to the Foundation Practices of Tibetan Buddhism* (2014) and *In Love with the World: A Monk's Journey Through the Bardos of Living and Dying* (2019), both of which she wrote with Yongey Mingyur Rinpoche.

LAWRENCE CHUA is a writer and producer, managing editor of *BOMB*, and a commentator for *Crossroads*, a weekly news magazine on National Public Radio (NPR). His writing has appeared in *The New York Times*, *The Village Voice*, *Rolling Stone*, *Transition*, and *Premiere*.

LISA JERVIS is an information systems consultant with a writer/editor past. She is a founder of *Bitch: Feminist Response to Pop Culture* and the author of *Cook Food: A Manualfesto for Easy, Healthy, Local Eating.* Her work is widely anthologized.

RANDY LOWENS, NOM DE PLUME DON JENNINGS was a former Workers' Solidarity Alliance member, a founding member of Atlanta's Capital Terminus Collective, and a supporter of Common Struggle-Libertarian Communist Federation. He died March 8, 2012, in Richmond, Kentucky.

SILAS HOUSE is the *New York Times* best-selling author of eight books whose work frequently appears in *The Atlantic* and *The New York Times.* He is a former commentator for NPR and his work has been widely published in journals and magazines such as *Time, The Advocate, Oxford American, Garden & Gun,* and many others. He has lectured internationally and is widely regarded as one of the major writers of the American South.

ABIGAIL BEREOLA is a writer and formerly the books editor at *The Rumpus.* Her work has appeared in *GQ, The Paris Review Daily, Shondaland,* and the *San Francisco Chronicle,* among other publications, as well as on *The Heart.*

THE LAST INTERVIEW SERIES

KURT COBAIN: THE LAST INTERVIEW AND OTHER CONVERSATIONS

"I am too stubborn ever to allow myself to compromise our music."

$17.99 / $23.99 CAN
978-1-68589-009-4
ebook: 978-1-68589-010-0

DIEGO MARADONA: THE LAST INTERVIEW AND OTHER CONVERSATIONS

"Football is the most beautiful sport in the world. If somebody makes a mistake, football need not pay for it. I made a mistake and I paid for it. But the ball does not stain."

$17.99 / $23.99 CAN
978-1-61219-973-3
ebook: 978-1-61219-974-0

JOAN DIDION: THE LAST INTERVIEW AND OTHER CONVERSATIONS

"I'm really tired of this angst business. It seems to me I'm as lively and cheerful as the next person. I laugh, I smile… but I write down what I see."

$17.99 / $23.99 CAN
978-1-68589-011-7
ebook: 978-1-68589-012-4

THE LAST INTERVIEW SERIES

JANET MALCOLM: THE LAST INTERVIEW AND OTHER CONVERSATIONS

"I did not set out to write about betrayal, but by writing about journalism, and photography I kept bumping into it."

$17.99 / $23.99 CAN
978-1-61219-968-9
ebook: 978-1-68589-012-4

JOHN LEWIS: THE LAST INTERVIEW AND OTHER CONVERSATIONS

"Get in good trouble, necessary trouble, and help redeem the soul of America."

$16.99 / $22.99 CAN
978-1-61219-962-7
ebook: 978-1-61219-963-4

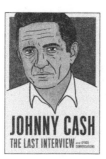

JOHNNY CASH: THE LAST INTERVIEW AND OTHER CONVERSATIONS

"I wouldn't let anybody influence me into thinking I was doing the wrong thing by singing about death, hell, and drugs. Cause I've always done that, and I always will."

$16.99 / $22.99 CAN
978-1-61219-893-4
ebook: 978-1-61219-894-1

THE LAST INTERVIEW SERIES

FRED ROGERS: THE LAST INTERVIEW AND OTHER CONVERSATIONS

"I think one of the greatest gifts you can give anybody is the gift of your honest self."

$16.99 / $22.99 CAN
978-1-61219-895-8
ebook: 978-1-61219-896-5

SHIRLEY CHISHOLM: THE LAST INTERVIEW AND OTHER CONVERSATIONS

"All I can say is that I'm a shaker-upper.
That's exactly what I am.

$16.99 / $22.99 CAN
978-1-61219-897-2
ebook: 978-1-61219-898-9

RUTH BADER GINSBURG : THE LAST INTERVIEW AND OTHER CONVERSATIONS

"No one ever expected me to go to law school. I was supposed to be a high school teacher, or how else could I earn a living?"

$17.99 / $23.99 CAN
978-1-61219-919-1
ebook: 978-1-61219-920-7

THE LAST INTERVIEW SERIES

MARILYN MONROE: THE LAST INTERVIEW AND OTHER CONVERSATIONS

"I'm so many people. They shock me sometimes.
I wish I was just me!"

$16.99 / $22.99 CAN
978-1-61219-877-4
ebook: 978-1-61219-878-1

FRIDA KAHLO: THE LAST INTERVIEW AND OTHER CONVERSATIONS

"The only thing I know is that I paint because I need to, and I paint always whatever passes through my head, without any other consideration."

$16.99 / $22.99 CAN
978-1-61219-875-0
ebook: 978-1-61219-876-7

TONI MORRISON: THE LAST INTERVIEW AND OTHER CONVERSATIONS

"Knowledge is what's important, you know?
Not the erasure, but the confrontation of it."

$16.99 / 22.99 CAN
978-1-61219-873-6
ebook: 978-1-61219-874-3

THE LAST INTERVIEW SERIES

GRAHAM GREENE: THE LAST INTERVIEW AND OTHER CONVERSATIONS

"I think to exclude politics from a novel is to exclude a whole aspect of life."

$16.99 / 22.99 CAN
978-1-61219-814-9
ebook: 978-1-61219-815-6

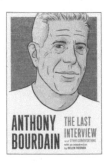

ANTHONY BOURDAIN: THE LAST INTERVIEW AND OTHER CONVERSATIONS

"We should feed our enemies Chicken McNuggets."

$17.99 / $23.99 CAN
978-1-61219-824-8
ebook: 978-1-61219-825-5

URSULA K. LE GUIN: THE LAST INTERVIEW AND OTHER CONVERSATIONS

"Resistance and change often begin in art. Very often in our art, the art of words."

$16.99 / $21.99 CAN
978-1-61219-779-1
ebook: 978-1-61219-780-7

THE LAST INTERVIEW SERIES

PRINCE: THE LAST INTERVIEW AND OTHER CONVERSATIONS

"That's what you want. Transcendence. When that happens—oh, boy."

$16.99 / $22.99 CAN
978-1-61219-745-6
ebook: 978-1-61219-746-3

JULIA CHILD: THE LAST INTERVIEW AND OTHER CONVERSATIONS

"I'm not a chef, I'm a teacher and a cook."

$16.99 / $22.99 CAN
978-1-61219-733-3
ebook: 978-1-61219-734-0

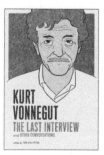

KURT VONNEGUT: THE LAST INTERVIEW

"I think it can be tremendously refreshing if a creator of literature has something on his mind other than the history of literature so far. Literature should not disappear up its own asshole, so to speak."

$15.95 / $17.95 CAN
978-1-61219-090-7
ebook: 978-1-61219-091-4

THE LAST INTERVIEW SERIES

JACQUES DERRIDA: THE LAST INTERVIEW
LEARNING TO LIVE FINALLY

"I am at war with myself, it's true, you couldn't possibly know to what extent... I say contradictory things that are, we might say, in real tension; they are what construct me, make me live, and will make me die."

translated by PASCAL-ANNE BRAULT and MICHAEL NAAS

$15.95 / $17.95 CAN
978-1-61219-094-5
ebook: 978-1-61219-032-7

ROBERTO BOLAÑO: THE LAST INTERVIEW

"Posthumous: It sounds like the name of a Roman gladiator, an unconquered gladiator. At least that's what poor Posthumous would like to believe. It gives him courage."

translated by SYBIL PEREZ and others

$15.95 / $17.95 CAN
978-1-61219-095-2
ebook: 978-1-61219-033-4

JORGE LUIS BORGES: THE LAST INTERVIEW

"Believe me: the benefits of blindness have been greatly exaggerated. If I could see, I would never leave the house, I'd stay indoors reading the many books that surround me."

translated by KIT MAUDE

$15.95 / $15.95 CAN
978-1-61219-204-8
ebook: 978-1-61219-205-5

THE LAST INTERVIEW SERIES

HANNAH ARENDT: THE LAST INTERVIEW

"There are no dangerous thoughts for the
simple reason that thinking itself is such a
dangerous enterprise."

$15.95 / $15.95 CAN
978-1-61219-311-3
ebook: 978-1-61219-312-0

RAY BRADBURY: THE LAST INTERVIEW

"You don't have to destroy books to
destroy a culture. Just get people to stop
reading them."

$15.95 / $15.95 CAN
978-1-61219-421-9
ebook: 978-1-61219-422-6

JAMES BALDWIN: THE LAST INTERVIEW

"You don't realize that you're intelligent
until it gets you into trouble."

$16.99 / $22.99 CAN
978-1-61219-400-4
ebook: 978-1-61219-401-1

THE LAST INTERVIEW SERIES

GABRIEL GÁRCIA MÁRQUEZ: THE LAST INTERVIEW

"The only thing the Nobel Prize is good for is not having to wait in line."

$15.95 / $15.95 CAN
978-1-61219-480-6
ebook: 978-1-61219-481-3

LOU REED: THE LAST INTERVIEW

"Hubert Selby. William Burroughs. Allen Ginsberg. Delmore Schwartz... I thought if you could do what those writers did and put it to drums and guitar, you'd have the greatest thing on earth."

$15.95 / $15.95 CAN
978-1-61219-478-3
ebook: 978-1-61219-479-0

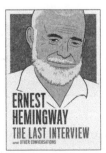

ERNEST HEMINGWAY: THE LAST INTERVIEW

"The most essential gift for a good writer is a built-in, shockproof shit detector."

$15.95 / $20.95 CAN
978-1-61219-522-3
ebook: 978-1-61219-523-0

THE LAST INTERVIEW SERIES

PHILIP K. DICK: THE LAST INTERVIEW

"The basic thing is, how frightened are you of chaos? And how happy are you with order?"

$15.95 / $20.95 CAN
978-1-61219-526-1
ebook: 978-1-61219-527-8

NORA EPHRON: THE LAST INTERVIEW

"You better *make* them care about what you think. It had better be quirky or perverse or thoughtful enough so that you hit some chord in them. Otherwise, it doesn't work."

$15.95 / $20.95 CAN
978-1-61219-524-7
ebook: 978-1-61219-525-4

JANE JACOBS: THE LAST INTERVIEW

"I would like it to be understood that all our human economic achievements have been done by ordinary people, not by exceptionally educated people, or by elites, or by supernatural forces."

$15.95 / $20.95 CAN
978-1-61219-534-6
ebook: 978-1-61219-535-3

THE LAST INTERVIEW SERIES

DAVID BOWIE: THE LAST INTERVIEW

"I have no time for glamour. It seems a ridiculous thing to strive for... A clean pair of shoes should serve quite well."

$16.99 / $22.99 CAN
978-1-61219-575-9
ebook: 978-1-61219-576-6

MARTIN LUTHER KING, JR.: THE LAST INTERVIEW

"Injustice anywhere is a threat to justice everywhere."

$15.99 / $21.99 CAN
978-1-61219-616-9
ebook: 978-1-61219-617-6

CHRISTOPHER HITCHENS: THE LAST INTERVIEW

"If someone says I'm doing this out of faith, I say, Why don't you do it out of conviction?"

$15.99 / $20.99 CAN
978-1-61219-672-5
ebook: 978-1-61219-673-2

THE LAST INTERVIEW SERIES

BILLIE HOLIDAY: THE LAST INTERVIEW AND OTHER CONVERSATIONS

"What comes out is what I feel. I hate straight singing."

$16.99 / $22.99 CAN
978-1-61219-674-9
ebook: 978-1-61219-675-6

HUNTER S. THOMPSON: THE LAST INTERVIEW

"I feel in the mood to write a long weird story—a tale so strange and terrible that it will change the brain of the normal reader forever."

$15.99 / $20.99 CAN
978-1-61219-693-0
ebook: 978-1-61219-694-7

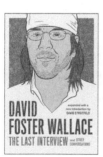

DAVID FOSTER WALLACE: THE LAST INTERVIEW AND OTHER CONVERSATIONS

"I'm a typical American. Half of me is dying to give myself away, and the other half is continually rebelling."

$16.99 / 21.99 CAN
978-1-61219-741-8
ebook: 978-1-61219-742-5